More Jazz

from

JUDY MURRAH

New Shapes & Great Ideas for
Wonderful Wearable Art

That Patchwork Place®

CREDITS

Editorial Director .... Kerry I. Hoffman
Technical Editor .... Barbara Weiland
Managing Editor .... Greg Sharp
Copy Editor .... Liz McGehee
Proofreader .... Melissa Riesland
Illustrator .... Laurel Strand
Illustration Assistant .... Lisa McKenney
Photographer .... Brent Kane
Design Director .... Judy Petry
Text and Cover Designer .... Kay Green
Production Assistant .... Shean Bemis

Special thanks to Molbak's, Columbia Winery, and Monte Villa Farmhouse for allowing us to use their establishments for photography.

More Jazz from Judy Murrah
©1996 by Judy Murrah
That Patchwork Place, Inc., PO Box 118, Bothell, WA 98041-0118 USA

Printed in Hong Kong
01 00 99 98 97 96   6 5 4 3 2 1

Library of Congress Cataloging-in-Publication Data
Murrah, Judy,
    More jazz / from Judy Murrah
            p. cm.
    ISBN 1-56477-135-0
    1. Coats. 2. Vests. 3. Patchwork—Patterns. 4. Quilted goods. I. Title.
TT535.M883 1996
746.46'0432—dc20   95-49842
                                                                CIP

MISSION STATEMENT

WE ARE DEDICATED TO PROVIDING QUALITY PRODUCTS AND SERVICES THAT INSPIRE CREATIVITY.

WE WORK TOGETHER TO ENRICH THE LIVES WE TOUCH.

That Patchwork Place is a financially responsible ESOP company.

Dedication

To my precious children:

Todd, who lights up my life along with his sweet wife, Julie;

Holly, my favorite shopping partner, who gives me energy; and

Troy, the strong, silent one, who shares my artistic spirit.

Acknowledgments

My deep appreciation goes to:

My editor, Barbara Weiland;

That Patchwork Place president, Nancy J. Martin;

Text and cover designer, Kay Green.

All my faithful students and giving teachers, whom I've enjoyed during the last two decades;

The loyal stores and guilds who have cared for and supported me and my students. A special thanks to Glenda Hulet at Sew What Bernina in Beaumont, Texas, (409) 892-7574. So many of you Jacket Jazz Groupies have told me she will go to any lengths to send you materials or tools you can't find to make a Jazz garment. She even hosts a monthly wearable-arts group, whose members make each of the Jacket Jazz Mystery Jackets. Thanks, Glenda. You are one in a million.

Also, thanks to Bernina of America, Inc.; Elna, Inc.; Omnigrid, Inc.; Fasco/Fabric Sales Co.; Hoffman California Fabrics; John Kaldor Fabricmaker USA, Ltd.; Fabri-Quilt, Inc.; Libas Ltd.; Lunn Fabrics; WFR Ribbon; Quilter's Resource, Inc.; The Leather Factory; and The Beadery.

Table of Contents

Jackets

Jazz Jr. and Mom Too 14

Mystery Jacket I—Out of This World . . 38

Vests for the Seasons

Tabards

Introduction

Since my first two books were published, many of you have sent me photos of your jackets and I've had the opportunity to see many of you in person wearing your jackets and vests. How much fun it has been to see you in your creations! You all look so proud and I'm proud of you. Thank you for the support and the love you have shown for my designs, and thank you too for your requests for more "Jazz."

More Jazz from Judy Murrah includes jackets, vests, and tabards. I wrote it using a format similar to the other Jazz books so those of you who have used the first two books can jump right in. However, even if you have made one or more jackets from my first two books, I recommend you read through "Let's Get Started" for review. Besides, there are a few new tidbits of information that didn't appear in the first books.

This book includes some garments that are a little different from those featured in the first books. If you've wanted to make a Jazz jacket for a child, you'll enjoy the child's jacket project. I've also included a basic vest with seasonal variations and, for those of you who love the Victorian theme, there's a jacket project featuring ribbons, linens, and laces. I think you'll enjoy making and wearing one of the tabards—a simple vestlike garment that's flattering on any figure.

These applications of the Jazz format are not new to me. In years past, I made embellished garments for my daughter until she started wearing designer clothes (that I didn't design!), and I often adorned clothing with whimsy to suit the season. As I explored quiltmaking techniques and made my first wearables, I embellished them with lots of linens, lace, and ribbon. When I became Director of Education for Quilts, Inc., however, I couldn't get the convention employees to take me seriously when I was dripping in lace, so the *Jacket Jazz* style evolved to replace my "too-feminine-for-business" look.

In this book, it has been fun to revisit some of my past working styles, creating new design options and providing you with a new garment shape—a simple tabard—plus a child's jacket to piece and patch and embellish to your heart's content. I hope you have even more fun with the projects in *More Jazz*!

Judy Murrah

Let's Get Started

Each of the adult jackets included in this book is based on the full-size patterns found in *Jacket Jazz* and *Jacket Jazz Encore*. Patterns for the child's jacket and the tabard are included on the pullout pattern at the back of this book. They are all basic enough for beginners. The shapes are simple and the sewing construction is easy; you'll spend the most time selecting fabric and creating the individual sections of each garment.

Choose your favorite project from the styles shown below. If you are a beginner, I recommend you start with one of the vests, since the patchwork pieces are a little less complex and there are no sleeves to set in. You'll have your vest done before you know it and you'll be ready for the next project. The tabard is also an easy project for beginners.

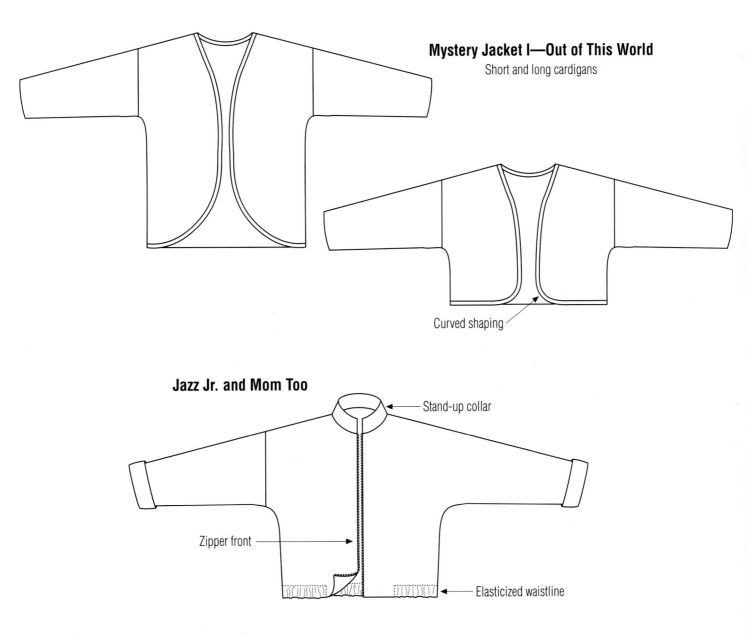

Mystery Jacket I—Out of This World
Short and long cardigans

Curved shaping

Jazz Jr. and Mom Too

Stand-up collar

Zipper front

Elasticized waistline

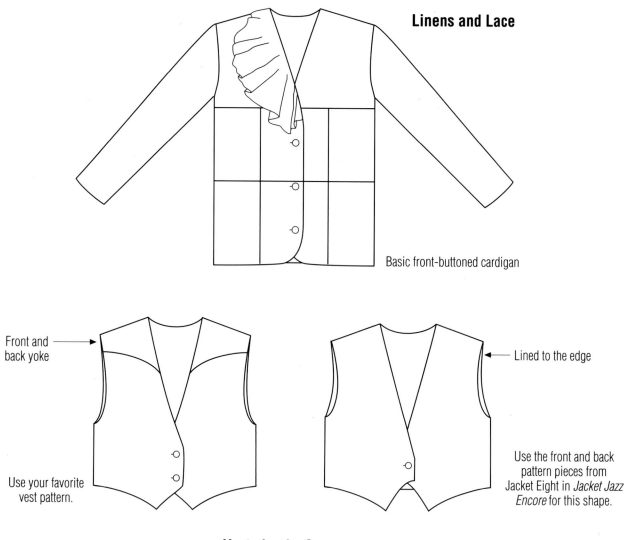

Linens and Lace

Basic front-buttoned cardigan

Front and back yoke

Lined to the edge

Use your favorite vest pattern.

Use the front and back pattern pieces from Jacket Eight in *Jacket Jazz Encore* for this shape.

Vests for the Seasons

NOTE: As my students experiment with these garments and the patchwork techniques, many of them play mix and match, choosing their favorite style and then applying the patchwork pieces of their choice. Some of the garments shown in the photos in this book are a result of this play, so they are not exactly like the pattern given here. If this approach appeals to you, you have my encouragement to play to your heart's content. However, I suggest that you follow one of my "recipes" for your first garment; then as you gain skill and confidence, you can create your own variations. You may want to use a favorite garment pattern for the foundation in place of those on the pullouts at the back of each of my three books.

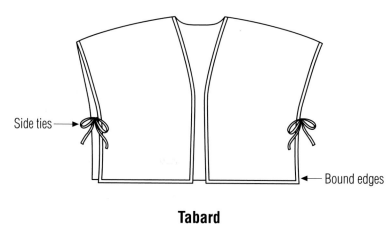

Side ties

Bound edges

Tabard

 Let's Get Started

✓Pattern Overview

The "Mystery Jacket" requires the pattern pieces for Jacket Five from *Jacket Jazz*. "And Mom Too" requires the pieces for Jacket Four from the same book. If you prefer, you may use a commercial pattern with similar styling. Look for a cardigan style with curved edges and dropped shoulders.

In *Jacket Jazz Encore*, you'll find the pattern pieces for Jacket Seven. Use these for the "Linens and Lace" jacket. Of course, you may substitute another favorite pattern for this jacket too, adapting it or the patchwork pieces as needed.

For the vest projects, choose a classic commercial pattern with a V-neck and pointed fronts. If you prefer, you can use the jacket front and back pattern pieces from Jacket Eight in *Jacket Jazz Encore*. However, this jacket is shorter and has a lower front neckline, so you may need to adapt the patchwork designs somewhat.

If you are using patterns from my previous books, follow the instructions on pages 10–11 in the appropriate book for tracing the required pattern pieces for each project. Be sure to trace the correct lines for your size; each pattern piece has cutting lines for five different sizes, from petite to extra large.

The child's jacket and the tabard pattern pieces are printed on the pullout pattern at the back of this book. The child's jacket has cutting lines for sizes 2, 4, 6, 8/10, and 12/14. The tabard is also multisized, with cutting lines marked for five sizes: Petite (6–8); Small (10–12); Medium (14–16); Large (18–20); and Extra Large (22–24). To choose your size, check the sizing chart below, using your bust measurement as a guide.

To preserve the original pattern pieces for later use, trace each pattern piece for the garment you are making onto tracing paper, following the lines for your size. Be sure to transfer all dots and notches for matching purposes.

All garment construction seam allowances are ½" wide unless otherwise noted. After tracing the pattern pieces for the garment you are making in the selected size, cut them from the tissue and pin together along the ½" seam lines. Try on to check the fit.

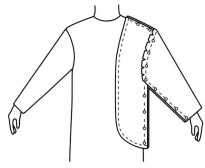

If you feel the pattern is too large, unpin the tissue, reposition the pieces over the master pattern, and trace the next smaller size.

You can also adjust the jacket fit once the patchwork pieces have been made and attached to the jacket foundation. Simply taper the side seams from the underarm down to the bottom edge of the garment if it seems too large. You may taper jacket sleeves too if you like a closer fit at the wrist.

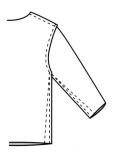

Taper side seams and underarm seams
for a closer fit at hips and wrist.

Adult Sizing Chart	Bust
Petite	29"–32"
Small	33"–35"
Medium	36"–38½"
Large	39½"–42½"
Extra Large	43"–46"

Children's Sizing Chart				
Size	2	4	6	8/10	12/14
Chest	21"	23"	25"	27"–28½"	30"–32"
Waist	20"	21"	22"	23½"–24½"	25½"–26½"
Hips	—	24"	26"	28"–30"	32"–34"

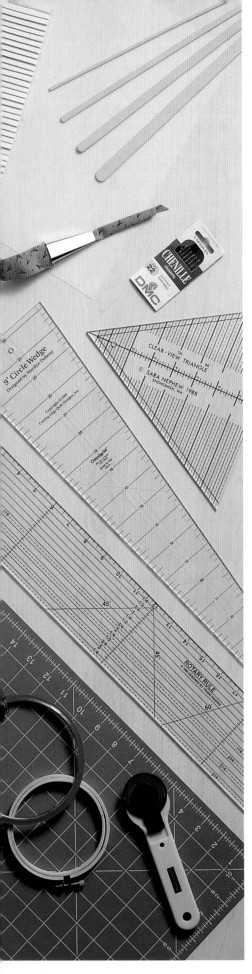

✓*Recipe for a Successful Garment*

Making one of my garments is a little like following a recipe. Directions are given for each garment from start to finish. There's no guessing what to do with the patchwork pieces after you make them. Follow the recipe, and the results will be a wonderful, wearable work of art.

1. Study the photos shown for each garment and select your favorite.
2. Before you go shopping, read through "General Materials" below. These are things you will need in order to make each of the garments.
3. After you decide which garment to make, refer to the "Shopping List" for that garment. Assemble all your supplies and materials before you begin.
4. Next, examine the photo of the garment you want to make in the section called "Construction at a Glance."
5. Be sure to save the scraps from your patchwork pieces to make a "Waste Not, Want Not" tabard (page 122), or use them to make a matching purse, following the directions on page 85 of *Jacket Jazz*. If you prefer to use them to make a zippered tote bag, refer to the directions for the Overnight Bag on page 35 in this book.

✓*General Materials*

No matter which of the garments you decide to make, you will need some special tools and materials.

TOOLS

In addition to a zigzag sewing machine and rotary-cutting equipment (cutter, mat, and your favorite rulers), you may need additional tools and supplies. Check the instructions for the garment you are making.

Be sure that your machine is in good working order and start with a fresh, sharp needle. You will be doing lots of stitching.

FABRICS AND NOTIONS

Garment Foundation Fabric—Cotton flannel or muslin. It is easier to work with flannel because your patchwork pieces will cling to it better than to muslin. However, flannel is heavier and warmer than muslin, so if you live in a warm climate, you may want to use muslin instead.

Garment Lining—Smooth, lightweight fabric. A silky lining fabric gives a more professional look and makes the garment easier to slip on and off. However, you might prefer a smooth cotton print for a coordinated look. Many times, I use large patchwork pieces left over from the garment to make the lining. The long version of the Mystery Jacket in this book has a different lining fabric in each section. That was fun to do, and it makes me happy to look inside the jacket. For the best of both worlds, use a cotton fabric in the jacket body and a silky lining in the sleeves.

Interfacing—Lightweight fusible interfacing. This adds support and prevents stretching around the neckline, front, and bottom edges of the garment. You will also need a pressing cloth and a copy of the manufacturer's fusing directions.

Large Pieces of Pattern Tracing Paper or Pattern Tracing Cloth—Using the pullout pattern at the back of the appropriate book, trace the pattern pieces in the proper size for the garment you are making onto tracing paper or cloth. (Tracing cloth is easier to use for a trial fitting as shown on page 9).

Upholstery Gimp, Braid, Bias Tape, Ribbon, or Other Flat, Decorative Trim—You will need several yards of ½"- to ⅝"-wide trim to cover the edges of some of the patchwork pieces after they are attached to the garment foundation. Check the shopping list for the garment you are making.

Shoulder Pads—I like raglan-style shoulder pads to support the weight of the jackets and to minimize my hip line. I insert them between the patchwork jacket and the lining, so they do not need to be covered. There is room in my jackets for shoulder pads that are ⅜" to ¾" thick, depending on your shoulders. The vests and tabards do not include shoulder pads since you may already have shoulder pads in the blouse or top you wear underneath.

Thread—Make sure you have thread in colors to match the trims, lining, and all fabrics you plan to use.

Fusible Web—You will need this for some of the patchwork pieces. (Check the "Shopping List" for the garment you are making.) Choose either a fusible web attached to a release paper or a web without release paper that requires the use of a Teflon® press cloth.

Decorative Beads—Check at your local fabric or crafts store, and watch for inexpensive jewelry items on sale. They are a great source of embellishment for wearable art.

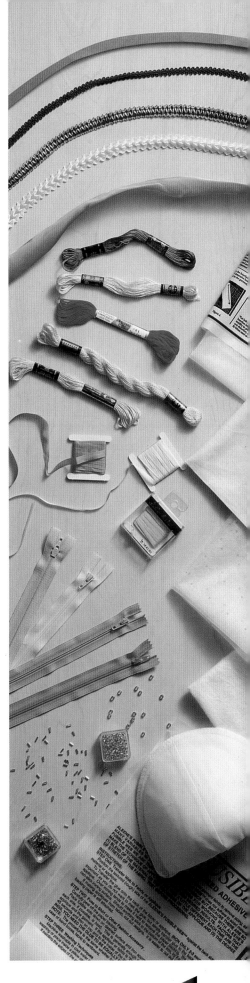

FABRIC SELECTION TIPS

Making one of the garments featured in this book is the perfect excuse to go shopping. It gives you a chance to use lots of fabrics in the colors you love. Start by choosing the garment you want to make and study the photos for fabric ideas. Specific suggestions for selecting fabric for each garment are included with the shopping lists. Take this book with you to the store for reference as you shop.

For easiest handling, select 100% cotton fabrics. I do not recommend prewashing any of the fabrics since they will lose body and will be more difficult to handle. If your fabrics have been prewashed, treat them with a little spray-on fabric finish to add body while you work with them.

Following are general guidelines for fabric selection that I share with my students in class. If you shop at a fabric store with knowledgeable staff, ask for their assistance too.

- Decide how you will wear your garment and the mood you wish to create. Will you wear it with denim skirts and jeans for casual, everyday attire, or with a skirt or dress for work? Would you rather make it for special occasions, such as holiday events? Choose fabrics that will create the desired effect.

  For casual wear or work, denims, solids, and calm prints are appropriate. For a dressier occasion, choose some fabrics that have a touch of gold or silver, plus multicolored prints, bright solids, and blacks. I use black in the majority of my garments so I can always wear them with black pants, skirts, or walking shorts. That makes traveling with these garments really easy.

  For a party or holiday garment, use lamé or other glamorous dressmaking fabrics. Select silkier trim with a finer texture than you might choose to mix with denim, and consider trims in gold or silver as well.

- At the fabric store, pull bolts of fabric that match the effect you wish to create. To get started, choose a theme print you love—one that has many colors. Then choose other fabrics to coordinate with the theme fabric. Choose as many as you can locate, even though you may have too many bolts in your initial stack. You may need to ask the store personnel to clear some counter space for you—if they're not too busy. (It's dangerous to make a stack of fifteen bolts on top of a fabric fixture, and it's difficult to remove bolts as you eliminate them without the "tower" falling!)

  Next, evaluate your selections. Is there an overall color pattern or theme? If there isn't a dominant fabric that contains many of the colors in the other fabrics you've chosen, look for one. You'll need to find the main fabric for your garment before you begin to add and eliminate others.

- Add or remove fabrics until you have the number required. For visual interest, try to include: a large print; a solid or two; small, tone-on-tone prints that look like solids from a distance; small and medium florals or geometric prints; and a stripe or a print with a definite pattern line to follow.

- Arrange fabrics with like colors together so they blend in a gradual transition, and evaluate again. Does color flow smoothly from one fabric to the next? Remove any that stick out—those that are too bright, too dull, too light, or too dark. Substitute one that makes a smoother transition. Be careful to include some value contrast. If the values are too similar, the resulting garment will be bland and unappealing.

- When you are pleased with your fabric selections, purchase the required yardage of each. Plan to use the fabric you love most for those parts of the garment that require the most yardage. If you are not entirely sure where you will use each piece, purchase a little extra of your favorites so you will have some design flexibility later. Don't forget that you can add other fabrics later if something just doesn't work the way you thought it would. Save what doesn't work for another project. As my mom said when I was a little girl, "Waste not, want not".

If you buy fabric you like when you see it, you can choose some or all of your fabrics at home. I have more fabric than I could use if I lived to be 100, but I love my stash. In the past, when I found a fabric I just couldn't leave behind in the store, I would buy a one-yard cut to add to my collection. Now that my storage space is getting crowded, I limit those have-to-have fabric purchases to $\frac{1}{2}$-yard cuts. With my plentiful fabric stash, I can plan a garment at midnight if I want to.

If you have a fabric collection too, try to select fabric from it first, then take the pieces you have chosen to the store and search for coordinating fill-ins. You're bound to find a fabric or two to add back into your stash while you are selecting fabrics for the garment you are planning that day. Oh, what fun!

✓ Garment Care

If you must clean your finished garment, be sure to ask the dry cleaner to clean and steam only. Pressing can ruin the beautiful patchwork and textures you've so carefully created on the surface of your garment. If you are careful to spot-clean your garment whenever necessary, you can keep dry cleaning to a minimum.

JACKETS

Jazz Jr. and Mom Too

- **Love and Kisses**
  (Options 1 and 2)

- **Zippity-Do-Da**

- **Lucy Locket's Pockets**

- **Ring-Around-the-Rosy Sleeves**

My Heart Belongs to Daddy

Zigzag Ribbon

Crisscross Hand-Couched Ribbon

Ribbon Twist

Gathered Rosettes

Peekaboo Points

✓ *Jazz Jr. and Mom Too Construction at a Glance*

**Lucy Locket's
Pockets**
(page 24)
→

Love and Kisses
Option 1
(page 19)

Zippity-Do-Da
(page 22)
←

Zigzag Ribbon
(page 28)

Peekaboo Points
(page 31)

Jazz Jr. by Judy Murrah.

Note: Jazz Jr. works for a boy, too, if you eliminate some of the fussy ribbon embellishments and "My Heart Belongs to Daddy."

**Love and Kisses,
Option 2 for adult sizes**
by Barbara Weiland.

PREPARATION

The Jazz Jr. pattern on the pullout at the back of this book includes the cutting lines for five different children's sizes. Trace the pattern pieces for the size you are making onto pattern tracing paper or cloth.

For the Adult version of Jazz Jr., use the jacket shape for Jacket Four found in the pullout section of *Jacket Jazz* or a commercial pattern with similar styling. When tracing the front and back pattern pieces, *trace the bottom-edge cutting line for Jacket 2 instead of for Jacket 4, unless you prefer a longer jacket.*

1. Cut 2 sleeves, 2 fronts, and 1 back from the foundation fabric. Repeat with the lining fabric unless you are planning to make a patchwork lining. (See step 1 of "Jacket Finishing" on page 31.) Cut 2 collars from the collar fabric and 1 from the interfacing.

2. Apply interfacing to the wrong side of 1 collar, following the manufacturer's directions. Set collar pieces aside. Cut 3"-wide strips of fusible interfacing and apply to the wrong side of the jacket at the center front, neckline, and bottom edges. To make straight strips fit around the curved neckline, slash and spread or make tiny wedge-shaped cutouts in the interfacing as you position and fuse it in place.

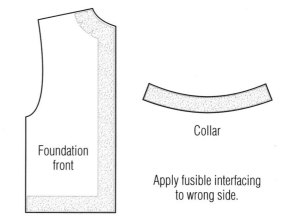

Foundation front

Collar

Apply fusible interfacing to wrong side.

3. Make and attach the patchwork pieces, pockets, and embellishments, following the directions on pages 19–31.

FABRIC SELECTION TIPS

- You will need a total of ten fabrics that work well together for the patchwork.
- Choose a border print or one that has obvious rows of motifs. If the jacket is for a child (or the child in you), look for one with child-like themes or motifs.
- Select coordinating prints, solids, stripes, and tone-on-tone prints.

Shopping List

All yardage requirements are based on 44"-wide fabrics, unless otherwise noted.

Note: The fabric yardages listed below for foundation, lining, and patchwork are enough for the Adult jacket with some left over. For the Jazz Jr. jacket, yardage includes enough for the lining and overnight bag as shown on page 35.

Jacket Foundation	2½ yds. cotton flannel or muslin
Jacket Lining	2½ yds. smooth cotton or silky lining fabric*
Patchwork and strips for back, fronts, and sleeves	½ yd. Fabric #1, a border print or theme fabric with rows of design motifs (See "Fabric Selection Tips" at left.)
	1 yd. each of Fabrics #2 and #3
	½ yd. each of Fabrics #4, #5, #6, #8, and #9
	¼ yd. each of Fabrics #7 and #10
Interfacing	¼ yd. (Jazz Jr.) or ⅜ yd. (Adult) lightweight, fusible interfacing
Fusible Web	Fusible web with paper backing for hearts
Shoulder Pads (Adult)	Raglan-style (⅜" to ¾" thick)
Elastic	1" wide and equal in length to waistline measurement for Jazz Jr.; twice waist measurement for Adult
Front Zipper	Separating zipper ½" shorter than the front edge of the jacket front pattern piece**
Zippity-Do-Da	4 zippers in lengths up to 12" and in assorted colors that coordinate with your fabric selections; zippers may have metal teeth or polyester or nylon coils
Zigzag Ribbon	2 yds. of ¼"-wide ribbon
Crisscross Hand-Couched Ribbon	1 yd. of ¼"-wide ribbon
	Pearl cotton or embroidery floss
Ribbon Twist	½ yd. each of 4 different colors of ¼"- wide ribbon
Gathered Rosettes	2 yds. of ¼"-wide ribbon
Other Trims	1 yd. of 1"-wide ribbon for folded ribbon at left shoulder
	3 yds. of narrow ready-made piping
	1¼ yds. of 1"-wide embroidered ribbon to alternate with fabric strips
Trinkets or Charms	6 for zipper pulls
Buttons for Pockets	3 (Jazz Jr.) or 4 (Adult) medium- to large-sized in fun designs
Buttons for Trim	4 or more for Jazz Jr.; 10 or more for Adult

   * If you prefer, you can wait to purchase lining until you have finished and applied all patchwork pieces to the jacket foundation. You may have enough leftovers to cut the lining pieces from the leftover patchwork fabrics.

   ** Buy a zipper that is longer than the front edge if you can't find one to match the jacket pattern piece length *minus* ½". For example, if your pattern piece measures 16½", buy an 18" or longer zipper. You will cut off the excess later.

✓Love and Kisses
(Options 1 and 2)

(Jacket Back)

MATERIALS

Jazz Jr. Sizes
2" x 42" strip each of Fabrics
   #1, #2, #4, and #5
7" x 42" strip of Fabric #3
3" x 42" strip of Fabric #6
2 buttons
1 yd. piping

Adult Sizes
4" x 42" strip each of Fabrics
   #1, #2, #4, and #5
14" x 42" strip of Fabric #3
6" x 42" strip of Fabric #6
6 buttons
2 yds. piping

DIRECTIONS

1. Cut the strips for the jacket size you are making (Jazz Jr. or Adult), cutting across the fabric width (crosswise grain).

Size	Jazz Jr. (Child)		Adult	
Fabric	No. of Strips	Size	No. of Strips	Size
#1	1	2" x 42"	2	2" x 42"
#2	1	2" x 42"	2	2" x 42"
#3	2	3½" x 42"	4	3½" x 42"
#4	1	2" x 42"	2	2" x 42"
#5	1	2" x 42"	2	2"x 42"

2. Arrange the strips and sew into Strip Units #1 and #2 as shown below, making sure to arrange them in the correct sequence. Use ¼"-wide seam allowances. Press seams in one direction in each unit.

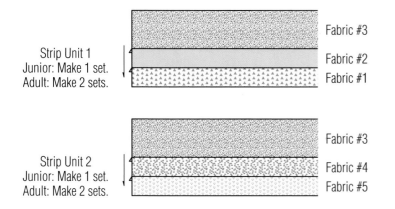

Strip Unit 1
Junior: Make 1 set.
Adult: Make 2 sets.

Fabric #3
Fabric #2
Fabric #1

Strip Unit 2
Junior: Make 1 set.
Adult: Make 2 sets.

Fabric #3
Fabric #4
Fabric #5

Note: If Fabric #1 or #5 is a directional print, stitch #1 so the design faces up and #5 so the design is upside down in the strip unit as shown in the units below.

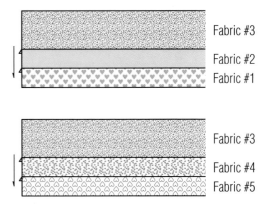

Fabric #3
Fabric #2
Fabric #1

Fabric #3
Fabric #4
Fabric #5

3. Crosscut the strip units into 6½" squares. Each strip unit should yield 6 squares. For the Jazz Jr. jacket, you should have 6 squares from each strip unit. For the Adult Jacket, you should have a total of 12 squares from each one.

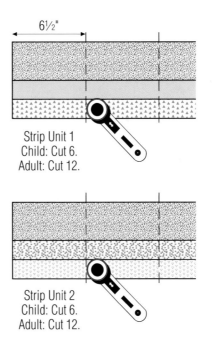

6½"

Strip Unit 1
Child: Cut 6.
Adult: Cut 12.

Strip Unit 2
Child: Cut 6.
Adult: Cut 12.

4. Stack the squares from Strip Unit 1 in 2 equal stacks, making sure that Fabric #3 is at the top of each square in each stack. Arrange the stacks side by side. Using a ruler and rotary cutter, cut the stacks diagonally so the cuts form a V from stack to stack as shown. Repeat with the squares from Strip Unit 2. Keep the stacks in this arrangement.

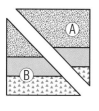

Strip Unit 1
Child: Cut 12 triangles.
Adult: Cut 24 triangles.

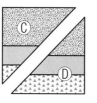

Strip Unit 2
Child: Cut 12 triangles.
Adult: Cut 24 triangles.

5. Using small pieces of masking tape, label the stacks of triangles as shown. Remember to remove the labels later.

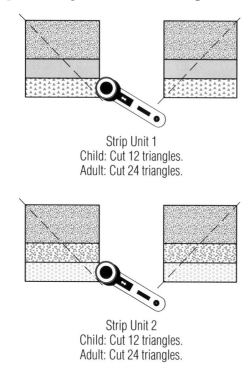

6. *For the Jazz Jr. jacket, Design Option #1:* Working from the bottom of each stack so you don't lose the tape labels, arrange the triangles as shown on a flat surface. Arrange 3 identical units.

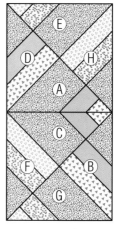

Design Option #1 (child sizes)
Make 3.

For the Adult jacket, Design Option #2: Working from the bottom of each stack, arrange the triangles as shown.

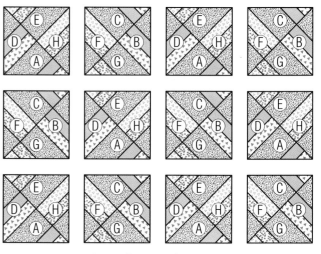

Design Option #2 (adult sizes)

Note: You can use Design Option #2 for the Jazz Jr. jacket by rearranging the squares. Sizes 4 and smaller require only 4 blocks. Use the remaining pieces from the smaller sizes for the Overnight Bag on page 35.

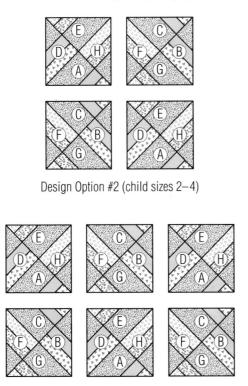

Design Option #2 (child sizes 2–4)

Design Option #2 (child sizes 6–10)

7. To assemble the units, sew each set of 2 adjacent triangles together, matching seams; press the seam in one direction. Sew the remaining 2 triangles together and press the seam in the opposite direction. Sew the pieced triangles together to complete each square.

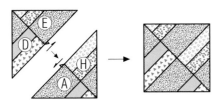

8. Sew the squares together in rows, then sew the rows together. Be careful to match seams at intersections. For Jazz Jr. size 4 and smaller, you will need only 4 squares, and for the larger children's sizes, you will use 6 squares. The Adult jacket requires a total of 12 squares, sewn into 4 vertical rows of 3 squares each.

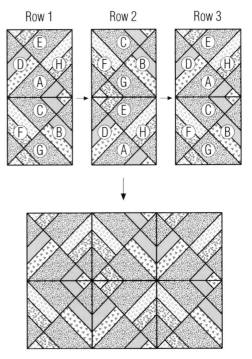

Row 1   Row 2   Row 3

Design Option #1 (child sizes 6–10)

Design Option #2 (adult sizes)

9. Place the foundation back right side up on a flat surface. With right side up, center the patchwork on the foundation, making sure that it covers the neckline and shoulder areas. Pin in place. Some foundation may show below the bottom edge of the patchwork, the amount depending on the size and length of the jacket you are making. *If the back length of your Adult jacket is 24" or less, the patchwork will cover the entire foundation.*

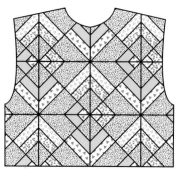

Adult jacket without strip of Fabric #6

10. *If foundation is exposed below the patchwork,* sew piping to the bottom edge of the patchwork, stitching through all layers. Use your zipper foot or a cording foot so you can stitch close to the piping cord.

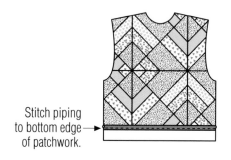

Stitch piping to bottom edge of patchwork.

Cut a strip of Fabric #6 that is slightly wider and longer than the exposed foundation. Place it right side down, aligning one raw edge with the bottom edge of the patchwork. Pin in place. Stitch close to the piping cord.

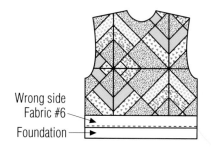

Wrong side Fabric #6

Foundation

11. Flip Fabric #6 down on top of the exposed foundation; press and pin in place. Turn foundation over and trim the excess patchwork even with the foundation edges. Stitch 1/8" from all raw edges.

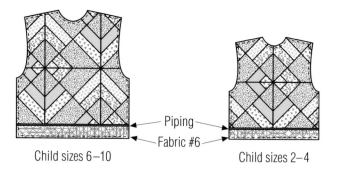

Child sizes 6–10   Child sizes 2–4

Piping
Fabric #6

12. You may add flat, decorative buttons where the squares meet in the completed patchwork. Besides adding design interest, they will hold the patchwork to the foundation and hide mistakes if seams don't match perfectly.

✓ *Zippity-Do-Da*

(Right Front)

MATERIALS

1/3 yd. (Jazz Jr.) or 1/2 yd. (Adult) of Fabric #2
Fabrics #1, #3, #4, #5, and #6 (see step-by-step directions for cutting information)
4 zippers, assorted colors, in lengths up to 12"
4 trinkets or charms for zipper pulls
Piping

DIRECTIONS

1. Place the right front foundation on a flat surface next to the jacket back, matching armhole and bottom edges. Mark the location of the top edge of Fabric #6 *on the wrong side of the front foundation.*
   (If you did not add a Fabric #6 strip to your jacket, ignore this step.)

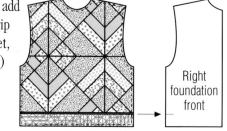

Right foundation front

Mark location on *wrong* side of foundation.

2. Cut a right front from Fabric #2. Place it right side up on the right front foundation, pin in place, and stitch ⅛" from the raw edges. When you unzip the zippers, this fabric will be the "pocket" lining that shows from behind the open zipper.

3. Divide the front into 6 angled sections of uneven widths. Sections #2, #3, #4, and #5 will be zippered pockets.

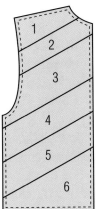

4. Select a section of Fabric #1 (border print) for Section #1. Cut a strip that is slightly larger than the space to be covered and turn under and press ¼" at the lower edge. Pin in place on the jacket foundation.

5. Choose a short zipper, and from a fabric that closely matches the color of the zipper tape, cut a 2"-long strip the same width as the zipper. Turn under ¼" at one short end and stitch it to the zipper above the zipper pull, using a zipper foot to get past the pull.

Fabric strip
extension

6. Tuck the zipper with fabric extension under the bottom edge of Strip #1 and position as desired, keeping the zipper pull at least 1" from the cut edge of the jacket foundation.
If the zipper does not reach to at least ½" from or to the armhole edge, add a fabric extension to the bottom of the zipper as you did above the zipper pull.

Pin the zipper in place with the pressed edge of Strip #1 about ¼" from the zipper teeth. Edgestitch in place through all layers.

Fabric strip
extension

Zipper
pull tab

Note: It's OK if zippers extend to or beyond the under-arm edge of the foundation. Leave excess zipper until you stitch the side seams. (See step 11 on page 24.)

7. Choose a fabric for the first zippered pocket, Strip #2. Cut a strip wide enough to reach across the entire front below the zipper, plus 1", and long enough to cover the lower edge of the zipper and the exposed foundation to the lower line of Section #2. Turn under and press ¼" along both long edges of Strip #2.

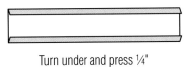

Turn under and press ¼"
at top and bottom edges.

8. Position the top edge of Strip #2 on the lower zipper tape, ¼" from the teeth. Pin the strip to the zipper tape only. *Lift the zipper away from the foundation.* Edgestitch Strip #2 to the zipper only. Position on the foundation; pin in place.

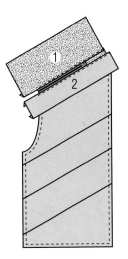

Note: If you wish, you can add Peekaboo Points, shown on page 31, to any of the zippered pocket sections before turning under the long raw edge that will be stitched to the lower half of the zipper.

8. Repeat steps 4–8 to add 3 more zippers and a total of 6 strips to the right front foundation. Alternate zipper colors and stagger the lengths. You may not need to add fabric extensions to very long zippers. Instead of adding a zipper between Strips #5 and #6, insert a piece of contrasting piping. *If you used extra long zippers, do not cut off the excess that extends at the underarm seam edge yet.*

Note: If you wish, you may add one of the ribbon embellishments shown on pages 29–30 to one of the pocket strips before applying it to the foundation.

9. Add a trinket or charm to each zipper pull.

10. If you added a Fabric #6 strip to the lower edge of the patchwork on the jacket back foundation, add a triangle of the same fabric to the lower underarm corner of the right jacket front. Position so the top edge begins at the mark you made (step 1) on the wrong side of the right front foundation. Apply the piece with piping, using the same method as you did on the jacket back.

11. Zip all zippers. Stitch 1/8" from the raw edges of the jacket front, *hand wheeling the fly wheel over any zippers that extend all the way to the edge in order to avoid breaking a needle.* Stitch a second time over the zipper ends. The stitches will act as the zipper stop. Trim fabric and zippers even with the foundation.

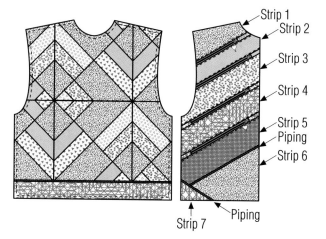

Strip 1
Strip 2
Strip 3
Strip 4
Strip 5
Piping
Strip 6
Strip 7
Piping

✔*Lucy Locket's Pockets*

(Left Front)

MATERIALS

1/3 yd. (Jazz Jr.) or 1/2 yd. (Adult) of Fabric #2
1/3 yd. each of Fabrics #4, #7, and #8
1/8 yd. each of Fabrics #1, #5, #6, and #9
Interfacing scraps for pocket flaps
3 (Jazz Jr.) or 4 (Adult) decorative buttons for flaps and
    embellishment
1 yd. of 1"-wide ribbon for folded ribbon at shoulder

DIRECTIONS

You will make 3 pockets, starting at the bottom and working toward the shoulder.

1. Cut a left front from Fabric #2. Place it, right side up, on the left front foundation; pin in place and stitch 1/8" from the raw edges. Divide the left front into 4 unequal sections, starting with Section #1 at the bottom as shown. Draw the divisions at the same angle you used for the zippered pockets on the right front.

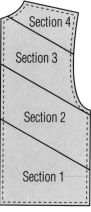

Section 4
Section 3
Section 2
Section 1

2. Cut a Fabric #4 strip wide enough to reach across the foundation along the top edge of Section #1, plus 1", and twice the length of the distance from the top line to the bottom corner at the front edge, plus 1". Fold the strip in half, *wrong sides together*, and press. Place the folded edge of the strip along the line and pin in place. Turn the foundation over and trim the folded strip even with the foundation.

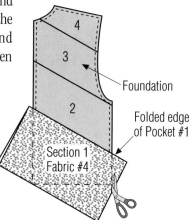

4
3
Foundation
2
Folded edge
of Pocket #1
Section 1
Fabric #4

3. Use the pattern for Pocket Flap #1 on the pullout. Lengthen or shorten it to match the measurement of the long edge of Pocket #1, minus ½" to allow for seam allowances at the front and side edges of the jacket. Cut 2 flaps from Fabric #6 and 1 from the fusible interfacing.

Cut apart and add tissue to lengthen.   Fold to shorten.

4. Apply the interfacing to the wrong side of one of the flaps. With right sides facing and using a ¼"-wide seam allowance, stitch the two flaps together, leaving the long edge unstitched. Clip the corners and turn right side out. Press.

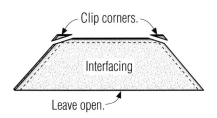

Clip corners.

Interfacing

Leave open.

5. Center the flap on the foundation, placing the raw edge ¼" *above* the folded edge of the pocket. Pin in place. At least ½" of the jacket should extend beyond each outer edge of the pocket flap.

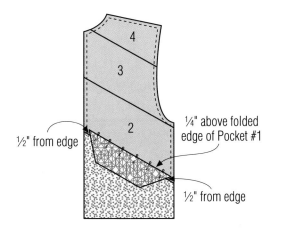

½" from edge

¼" above folded edge of Pocket #1

½" from edge

6. Using Fabric #7, cut, fold, and press a strip for the second pocket. With raw edges matching and using a ¼"-wide seam allowance, sew the second pocket in place on top of Pocket Flap #1. Take care not to catch the folded upper edge of Pocket #1 in the stitching. Flip Pocket #2 up onto the foundation; press and pin in place.

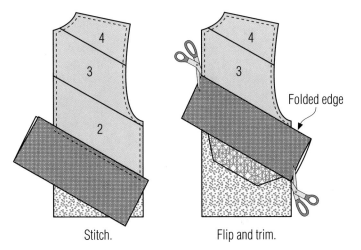

Folded edge

Stitch.   Flip and trim.

7. Using Pocket Flap #2 on the pullout, adjust as needed to fit across the upper edge of Pocket #2 and reach almost to the bottom of the pocket. Cut 2 flaps from Fabric #1 and 1 from interfacing. Apply interfacing and prepare the flap as you did the first one, leaving the long edge unstitched. Turn, press, position, and stitch to the foundation above Pocket #2 as you did Pocket Flap #1. Refer to the illustration following step 9 on page 26.

8. Using Fabric #8, cut, fold, and press a strip for the third pocket. With raw edges matching and using a ¼"-wide seam allowance, sew the third pocket in place on top of Pocket Flap #2. Do not catch the folded upper edge of Pocket #2 in the stitching. Using Pocket Flap #3 on the pullout, adjust as needed, cut flaps from Fabric #5 and interfacing, and prepare the flap as you did the first two. Stitch the flap in place above Pocket #3 as you did the first two.

9. Add a piece of Fabric #9 to the top edge of the upper flap, using the same method used to attach the pockets. Flip Fabric #9 onto the foundation; press and pin in place. Turn the foundation over, stitch ⅛" from all edges, and trim all edges even with the foundation.

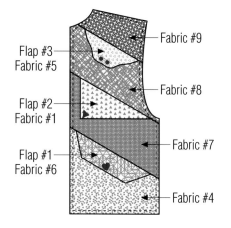

Fabric #9
Flap #3
Fabric #5
Fabric #8
Flap #2
Fabric #1
Fabric #7
Flap #1
Fabric #6
Fabric #4

10. Cut a 1" x 4" cardboard box-pleating guide or use a 1" x 6" C-Thru® Ruler if you have one. Place the strip or ruler 2" in from one end of the 1"-wide ribbon. Fold the ribbon back on top of the cardboard to the opposite edge of the guide, then back on top of itself. Carefully remove the cardboard and pin the 3 layers of folded ribbon together.

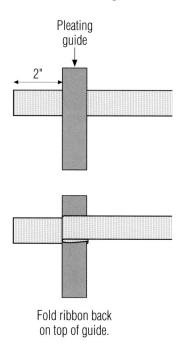

Pleating guide

2"

Fold ribbon back on top of guide.

11. Place the cardboard strip under the ribbon next to the first inner fold. Wrap ribbon under the guide to meet the inner fold, then fold back to complete 1 box pleat.

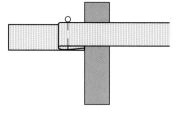

Fold ribbon back on top of guide.

Slide the cardboard out and pin. You should have a 2"-long box pleat on the top side of the ribbon.

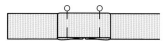

Box pleat

12. Continue making box pleats until you have enough folded ribbon to fit along the shoulder edge of the jacket front. You will probably need 3 pleats for the Jazz Jr. sizes and 4 for the Adult sizes. Pin the folded ribbon in place on Fabric #9 near the shoulder seam. Machine stitch down the center of the pleats through all layers, using matching thread.

Machine stitch down center of folded ribbon.

13. Pinch the edges of each pleat together in the center and, using matching thread, whipstitch as shown.

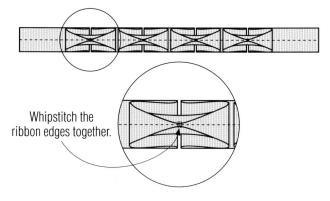

Whipstitch the ribbon edges together.

14. Add a row of buttons below the ribbon and a strip of embroidered ribbon if desired (and if there is space for it).

✓ Ring-Around-the-Rosy Sleeves

(Both Sleeves)

Make matching sleeves for this jacket, using a variety of strips from your fabric leftovers. You will need seven different fabrics. Adjust the strip widths for the size you are making and to accommodate design motifs from your fabrics, particularly rows of motifs from your border print, Fabric #1. Directions are included for six embellishment techniques to add to the strips. You may use any of these to further embellish the jacket fronts if you wish.

My Heart Belongs to Daddy

MATERIALS

1 strip of fabric, 5½" wide and slightly longer than widest part of sleeve, for hearts

2 strips of fabric of your choice; width and length depend on where you place them (see steps 7 and 8)

Fusible web with paper backing

DIRECTIONS

1. Fold 1 fabric strip in half lengthwise with *wrong sides together*. Stitch 1½" from the fold. Using a removable marking pencil or a sharp pencil, draw a faint line 1" from stitching as shown.

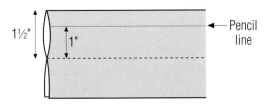

Draw a faint line 1" from stitching.

2. Open out the raw edges of the strip, centering the drawn line over the seam line to create an uneven box pleat that is ½" wide above the seam line and 1" wide below it. Press. Using matching thread, stitch on the drawn line. Press.

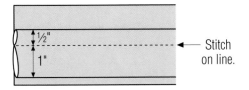

3. Cut a ¾"-wide strip of paper-backed fusible web the length of the pleated strip. Following the manufacturer's directions, apply fusible web to the underside of the 1"-wide half of the pleat. Cut a ⅜"-wide strip of fusible web and apply to the underside of the narrower half of the pleat. *Do not remove the backing paper yet.*

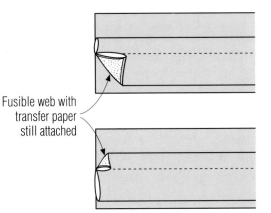

Fusible web with transfer paper still attached

4. Mark cutting lines from fold to fold at 2" intervals. Go back and mark halfway between each mark along the narrower half of the pleat only. Lifting the folded edge with the point of your scissors, cut to the stitching on the marked lines.

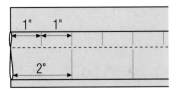

Mark the tucks for cutting.

5. Turn down the seam allowance behind the narrower half of the pleat and place the strip on your ironing board. Removing the backing paper one section at a time, turn in the folded edge of each section to form points. Press, making sure that the fusible web adheres. Repeat with all remaining cut edges along the narrower half of the pleat to make the heart points.

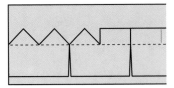

Fold and press to make heart points.

6. Repeat step 5 to form the lower point of each heart. Press. Stitch ⅛" above and below the center seam line. The heart strips will be Strip #2 on each sleeve.

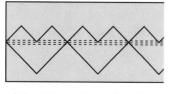

Stitch ⅛" away from original line
of stitching on both sides.

7. Choose 2 fabrics that contrast with the heart fabric. Use 1 of the fabrics for Strip #1 to cover the upper portion of each sleeve foundation, ending 2" to 3" below the underarm corners. Turn under and press ¼" at the lower edge of each strip. Tuck the top raw edge of a heart strip under the turned edge of each Strip #1 and pin in place. Edgestitch, holding the heart points out of the way of the stitching. Stitch ⅛" from the outer edges of the foundation.

8. Cut a strip of the second contrasting fabric to place below the hearts for Strip #3, cutting it the desired width. Turn under and press ¼" on one long edge. Position the turned edge on top of the lower edge of the heart strip; pin. Edgestitch, holding points out of the way.

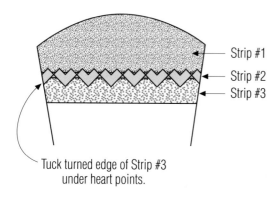

Strip #1
Strip #2
Strip #3

Tuck turned edge of Strip #3
under heart points.

Zigzag Ribbon

MATERIALS

Fabric for Strip #4
2 yds. of ¼"-wide ribbon

DIRECTIONS

1. Cut 2 strips from the desired fabric for Strip #4. Place a strip on each sleeve face down at the bottom edge of Strip #3, aligning raw edges. Stitch ¼" from the raw edge. Flip the strip down onto the foundation; press and pin. Trim excess fabric strip even with the foundation raw edges.

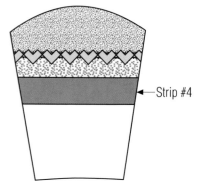

Strip #4

2. Beginning on the left side of the sleeve, position the ribbon at the top of Strip #3, and to the left of the first heart. Bring the ribbon down to the bottom of Strip #3, in line with the point of the heart tip above it. Stitch along one edge of the ribbon. *Leave the sewing-machine needle in the fabric and ribbon.*

3. Lift the presser foot and pivot the fabric, folding the ribbon to take it to the opposite edge of Strip #3, zigzag fashion. The ribbon should be to the right of the first heart. Stitch the next portion of the ribbon. Leave the needle in the ribbon and fabric. Pivot and repeat steps 2 and 3 until you reach the end of the strip. Stitch the free edge of the ribbon in place, pivoting as necessary.

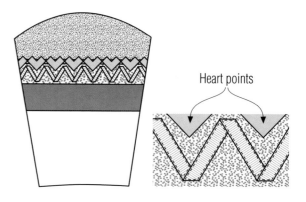

Heart points

Crisscross Hand-Couched Ribbon

MATERIALS

1 yd. of ¼"-wide ribbon

Pearl cotton or embroidery floss

If you wish to embellish Strip #4, hand couch a piece of plain ribbon in place or choose a decorative ribbon and edgestitch it in place by machine.

DIRECTIONS

1. Pin a piece of ribbon to Strip #4.
2. Thread a needle with floss or pearl cotton thread and anchor the short end of the ribbon at the raw edge of the sleeve with a few backstitches. Do a catch stitch over the ribbon to hold it in place, catching the ribbon edges in the backstitches. Referring to the illustration, bring the needle up at 1, then take a backstitch in the direction of the arrow at 2. Bring the thread over the ribbon to the right and take a backstitch at 3. Continue in the same manner until you reach the end of the ribbon, being careful to space the stitches evenly. Anchor the end of the ribbon with a few backstitches.

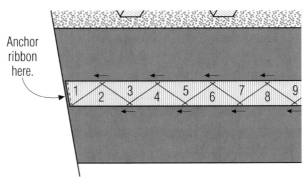

Catch stitch over ribbon centered on Strip #4.
Arrows indicate stitching direction.

Ribbon Twist

MATERIALS

Fabric for Strip #5 (at least 2" wide)

½ yd. each of 4 different colors of ¼"-wide ribbon

2 yds. piping

DIRECTIONS

1. Cut 2 strips from the fabric for Strip #5 in the desired width.
2. Cut lengths of each ribbon, making them each ½" longer than the cut width of Strip #5. Pin ribbon lengths to the top edge of each Strip #5, spacing them at 1" to 1½" intervals. Twist each ribbon once and pin the bottom edge to the bottom edge of Strip #5. Stitch ⅛" from the long raw edges to secure the ribbons. Remove the pins.
3. Add piping to the top and bottom raw edges of each Ribbon Twist strip. Turn seam allowances to the wrong side; press.

Add piping
to Strip #5.

4. Pin the Ribbon Twist strips so piping rests ¼" above the bottom raw edge of Strip #4. Stitch in-the-ditch between the piping and the upper edge of the strip only.

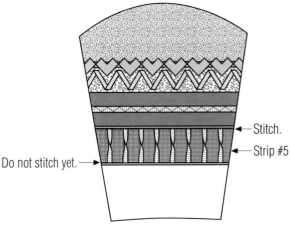

Add Strip #5 to sleeve.

Gathered Rosettes

MATERIALS

Fabric for Strip #6
Fabric for Strip #7
2 yds. of ¼"-wide ribbon

DIRECTIONS

1. Cut 2 strips from the fabric for Strip #6. Place the top ¼" of each strip under the bottom edge of a Strip #5 on each sleeve. Stitch in-the-ditch between the piping and Fabric #5.

2. Cut the ribbon into 2 equal lengths. Working on one sleeve at a time, pin the short end of 1 piece of ribbon to Strip #6, positioning it at the desired location in the strip. Thread a needle with sewing thread, double, and knot. Anchor the ribbon to the sleeve with 2 backstitches. After inserting the needle for the second stitch, bring the needle up from the back of the fabric approximately 1" from the stitches. Backstitch again.

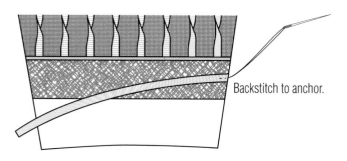

Backstitch to anchor.

3. Lift the ribbon away from the sleeve and make a 1½"-long row of stitches through the center of the ribbon only.

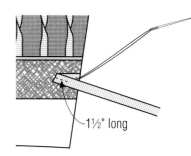

1½" long

4. Draw the thread up tightly to make a tiny gathered rosette. Take 2 or 3 stitches close to the first anchor stitch through ribbon and fabric. Insert the needle in the fabric and bring it out on the back side of the sleeve. Move forward 1", bring the needle up, and anchor the ribbon with 2 more backstitches.

5. Repeat steps 3 and 4 to make the next rosette, continuing until you reach the other edge of the sleeve.

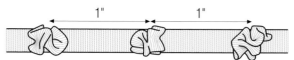

1"   1"

Draw up gathers to make roses, then tack to fabric strip.

6. Cut 2 strips of the desired fabric for Strip #7 and sew 1 to the bottom edge of Strip #6 on each sleeve, using the stitch-and-flip method. Turn the sleeves over and trim excess fabrics even with the foundation. Stitch ⅛" from the raw edges all the way around each sleeve.

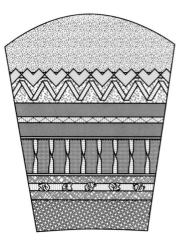

Note: If you want to wear the sleeves rolled up, do not add any embellishment to this strip. Otherwise, you can add one of the embellishments already described or Peekaboo Points, described on opposite page.

Peekaboo Points

If you wish, use this technique on one of the front pockets, on a sleeve, and/or on the overnight bag.

MATERIALS

2" x 42" strip of fabric that contrasts with the fabric strip to which it will be added
Beads, charms, or trinkets (optional)

DIRECTIONS

1. Cut the 2"-wide strip to match the length of the area you are embellishing. Draw a line $\frac{1}{4}$" from one long edge. Cut to the line at 3" intervals along the length of the strip.

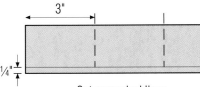

Cut on marked lines.

2. Fold each rectangle segment in half, right sides together. Stitch $\frac{1}{4}$" from the short end. Trim across the corner. Turn each point right side out and press flat.

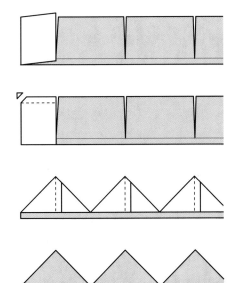

Turn points right side out.

3. Place the raw edge even with the top edge of a fabric strip and stitch $\frac{1}{8}$" from the raw edges, then add the fabric strip to the desired location on the garment. Add beads, charms, or trinkets to the points if desired.

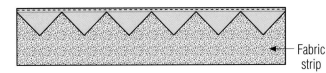

Fabric strip

✓Jacket Finishing

Use $\frac{1}{2}$"-wide seam allowances.

Note: To simplify the illustrations, patchwork is not shown.

1. Use the completed fronts, back, and sleeves as patterns for cutting the lining pieces from fabric leftovers or a single fabric. Place patchwork-covered jacket pieces, right side up, on the wrong side of the lining; pin in place and cut out.

2. Sew the jacket fronts to the back at the shoulder seams. Press the seams open. Stitch the sleeves to the jacket armholes, piping the seams if desired. Press the seams open.

Stitch shoulder seams.

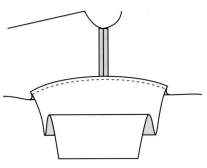

Add sleeves.

3. With right sides together, stitch the continuous underarm seam of the jacket and sleeve; press seams open. When stitching the right side seam, you may be stitching over the ends of zippers. *When you reach the zipper teeth, stop and use your hand to rotate the flywheel so you stitch slowly and don't break a needle.* For added security, you may want to stitch over the zipper teeth areas a second time, on top of the first stitching. Sew shoulder pads in place in adult-size jacket.

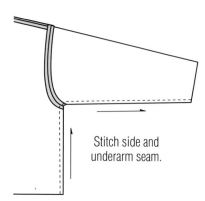

Stitch side and underarm seam.

4. Repeat steps 2 and 3 with the lining, ignoring the reference to the zippers and the shoulder pads.
5. Turn under and press $1/2$" on the long edge of the collar piece without interfacing. With right sides facing, stitch the 2 collar pieces together, leaving the bottom edge open. Trim the seams to $1/4$" and trim the corners to reduce bulk. Turn right side out and press. Set aside.

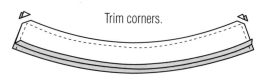

Trim corners.

Turn under $1/2$" on one collar piece.

6. With right sides together, pin the lining to the jacket along the bottom raw edges. Stitch. Trim the seam to $1/4$", turn right side out, and press. Tuck the sleeve linings into the sleeves. Machine baste the lining to the jacket along the neckline, $3/8$" from the raw edge.
7. Decide how much elastic you want in the bottom edge of the jacket. It should extend at least to the side seams as it does in Jacket Four from *Jacket Jazz,* but if you wish, you can have elastic in the fronts too, ending $2^{1}/2$" from the cut edges of the jacket fronts.

   Using matching thread, edgestitch $1/4$" from the folded edge, beginning and ending where you want the elastic to end on the fronts (or at the side seams). Stitch again $1^{1}/8$" from the first stitching. *For the Adult sizes only, stitch $1^{1}/8$" away from the second row of stitching so you have a casing that will hold 2 pieces of elastic.*

Lining

Stitch through both layers to form casing(s) for elastic.

8. Cut 2 pieces of 1"-wide elastic (1 piece for Jazz Jr.), making them 1" shorter than the casing measurement at the bottom edge of the jacket. Thread the elastic through the casings and pin in place at the side seams or fronts, leaving $1/4$" of elastic extending beyond each end of the casing stitching. On the right side of the jacket, stitch across the ends of the casing opening, catching the elastic in the stitching. Stitch a second time for reinforcment. Adjust the gathers evenly across the jacket bottom.

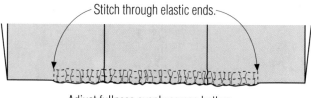

Stitch through elastic ends.

Adjust fullness evenly across bottom.

9. Stitch $5/8$" from the front raw edges through the jacket and lining layers. Trim $1/2$" from each front edge, leaving $1/8$" of fabric extending beyond the stitching line.

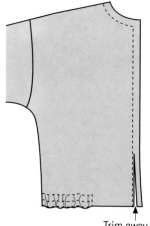

Trim away $1/2$".

10. Using leftover fabric, cut 2 strips of 2"-wide fabric, each the length of the jacket front edge plus $1/2$". Fold each one in half lengthwise with wrong sides together and press to make the binding strips.

11. Pin a folded binding strip to the lining side of the jacket, keeping raw edges even and the excess strip below the bottom edge of the jacket. Stitch ¼" from raw edges.

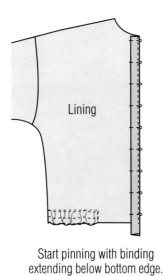

Start pinning with binding
extending below bottom edge.

12. Fold the binding away from the jacket and press. Fold the end of the strip up over the bottom edge, then turn the binding over the seam edges onto the jacket front. Pin the folded edge in place. Edgestitch in place through all layers.

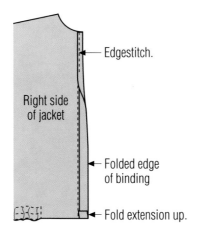

Right side of jacket

Edgestitch.

Folded edge of binding

Fold extension up.

13. Place the closed separating zipper under the bound front edges with the zipper teeth exposed. Pin or baste in place, *making sure the bottom stop is at the bottom edge of the jacket fronts and any excess zipper length extends above the top edge of the neckline.* Stitch in-the-ditch through all layers next to the folded edge of the binding. The zipper tape will show on the lining side of the jacket.

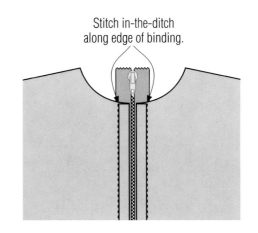

Stitch in-the-ditch along edge of binding.

14. *Unzip the zipper.* Pin the interfaced half of the collar to the neckline with right sides together and front edges even. Stitch, being careful to move the flywheel by hand if you must stitch over zipper teeth, to avoid breaking the needle.

15. Trim the seam to ¼", cutting away excess zipper, and press the collar toward the trimmed seam. Slipstitch the folded edge of the collar in place along the stitching line on the inside of the jacket.

Unzip the zipper.

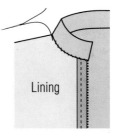

Lining

Slipstitch collar to lining.

16. With the sleeve linings pushed up out of the way, stitch piping to the bottom edge of each sleeve, overlapping as shown. Turn the seam allowance toward the sleeve. Turn under and press ¼" around the bottom edge of each sleeve lining; press. Stitch the pressed edge of the lining to the sleeve by hand or machine. If desired, turn the sleeve up to create a cuff that reveals the lining fabric.

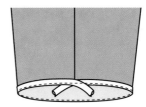

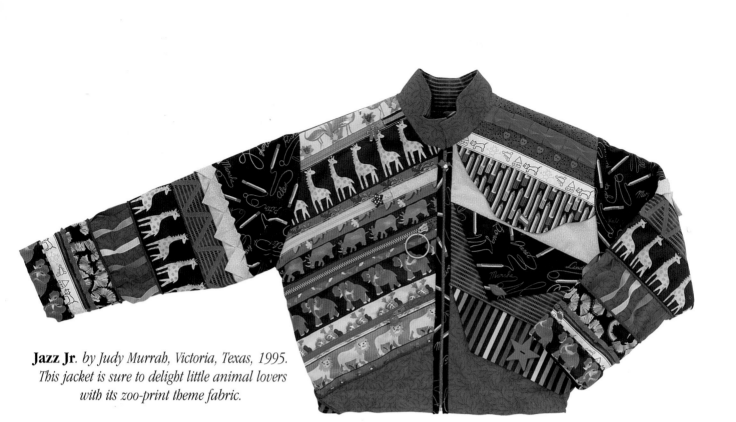

Jazz Jr. *by Judy Murrah, Victoria, Texas, 1995.*
This jacket is sure to delight little animal lovers
with its zoo-print theme fabric.

Overnight Bag

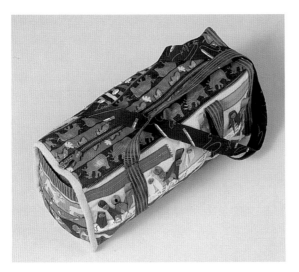

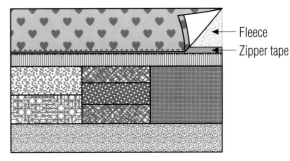

Tuck leftover zipper pieces under
fabric strips for interesting "piping."

What child wouldn't love to have a special bag like this to hold his or her things for an overnight visit to Grandma's house?

Topstitch short zipper pieces to strips, placing them so the cut ends will be caught in a seam at the edges.

MATERIALS

15" x 23" piece of polyester fleece for bag foundation
15" x 23" of fabric for lining
Fabric leftovers for patchwork
2 strips of desired fabric, each 3" x 37", for straps
2 strips of fusible interfacing, each 2½" x 37", for straps
15" or longer zipper
1 package purchased double-fold bias tape, or make your own from fabric scraps
Assorted buttons
Ribbon leftovers

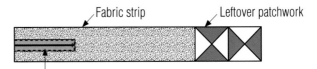

Topstitch short zipper leftovers to fabric strips.

For buttoned ribbon embellishments, fold small pieces of ribbon in half and sew to the foundation through the holes of buttons. Trim ribbon ends at an angle to prevent raveling.

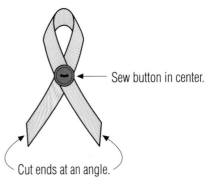

Sew button in center.

Cut ends at an angle.

DIRECTIONS

Use the bag-end pattern on the pullout.

1. Cover the fleece foundation with strips of fabric, using the stitch-and-flip method you used for the jacket sections. Embellish with zippers and ribbons. Add trims and trinkets as desired. Use leftover zipper pieces as piping between the seams of two of the strips as shown above right.

2. Center a strip of fusible interfacing on the wrong side of each strap; fuse. Turn under and press ¼" on each long edge. Fold each strap in half lengthwise, right sides together; stitch ¼" from each short end. Trim corners, turn, and press.

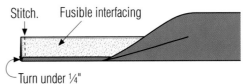

Stitch.   Fusible interfacing

Turn under ¼"
on each long edge.

3. Fold each strip in half lengthwise, aligning folded edges; edgestitch through all layers along both long edges.

Fold

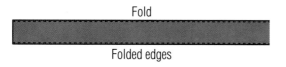

Folded edges

4. Pin straps to the patchwork 3" from the long edges and 7" from the short edges as shown. Stitch for 3½" along each strap side and across each bottom edge.

Stitch for 3½".

3½"

3"

7"

Patchwork

15"

23"

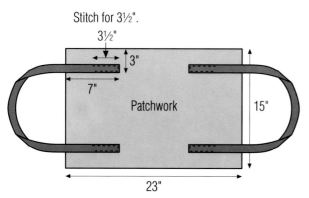

5. Pin the zipper to one edge of the patchwork as shown, *with right sides together and zipper zipped*. Align the raw edge of the fabric with the edge of the zipper tape. Using a zipper foot, stitch ¼" from the edge of the zipper tape.

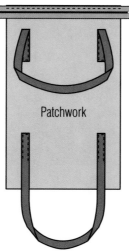

Patchwork

Note: The zipper slider and the upper end of the zipper coil may extend beyond the patchwork piece.

6. Repeat step 5 at the opposite end of the patchwork.

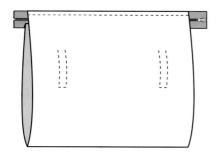

7. *Unzip the zipper.* Pin the lining to the patchwork, right sides together, with the zipper sandwiched between the two layers of fabric. Working from the wrong side of the patchwork, stitch on top of the previous zipper stitching. Repeat with the other end of the lining.

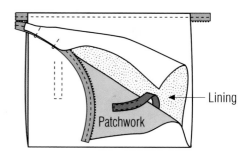

Lining

Patchwork

8. Using the pattern on page 37, cut 2 tabs from the desired fabric. Stitch with right sides together, leaving the straight end open. Clip the point, turn, and press. Topstitch ¼" from the finished edges. Center and pin the tab over the zipper end of the bag, aligning the raw edges. Stitch ¼" from raw edges.

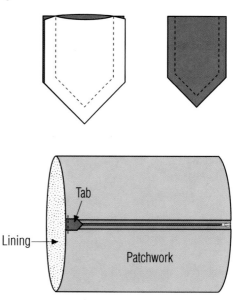

Tab

Lining

Patchwork

9. Using the bag-end pattern piece on the pullout, cut 2 each of fleece, bag fabric, and lining fabric. Place each end-lining piece face down on a flat surface; place fleece on top, followed by the bag end, right side up. Baste ¼" from the edges.

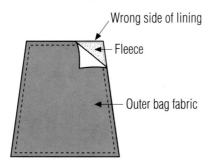

Wrong side of lining

Fleece

Outer bag fabric

10. For a pocket at each end of the bag, cut 2 pieces, each 7" x 13", from the desired fabrics. Fold each piece in half with wrong sides together so each measures 6½" x 7". Position a pocket on each bag end ¾" from the top edge. Pin in place. Turn over and trim excess pocket even with the raw edges of the bag end. Stitch ¼" from the raw edges.

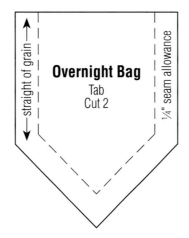

Bag end

¾"

Pocket

11. Stitch a scant ⅜" from the raw edges of the bag. Clip to the stitching 2" and 8" from the zipper teeth on each bag half.

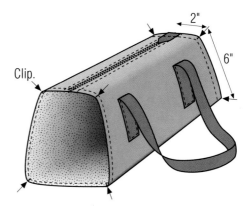

2"

6"

Clip.

12. Pin a bag end to each open end of the bag, keeping the end lining next to the bag lining, raw edges even, and the corners at the clips. Stitch ⅜" from the raw edges and trim seams to ¼". Bind the raw edges with double-fold bias tape. Add a trinket to the zipper pull tab. Pack up for a trip to Grandma's house!

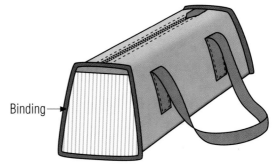

Binding

Encase raw edges with double bias.

Overnight Bag
Tab
Cut 2

straight of grain

¼" seam allowance

Mystery Jacket 1* — Out of This World

- **Trip Around the World**
- **Couched Tucks**
- **Pleated Spaceships**
- **Mystery Jazz Squares**

  - *Folded Star Block*
  - *Hawaiian Appliqué Block*
  - *String-Pieced Square Block*
  - *Cathedral Window Block*
  - *Log Cabin Borders*

- **Yo-yos**
- **Woven String Strips**
- **Woven Square Strips**

Why is this jacket called Mystery Jacket 1? I offer jacket classes by correspondence course through the mail. Since participants do not see a finished sample, the jacket is a mystery that unravels, month by month. I retired the first jacket in this series so that I could include it in this book. If you are interested in information about my current Mystery Jacket, send a self-addressed, stamped envelope to my attention at 109 Pasadena Drive, Victoria, TX 77904.

If you haven't tried a short version of the Jazz Jackets, try this one. It's one of my favorites and it's flattering on most figure types!

✓Out of This World Construction at a Glance

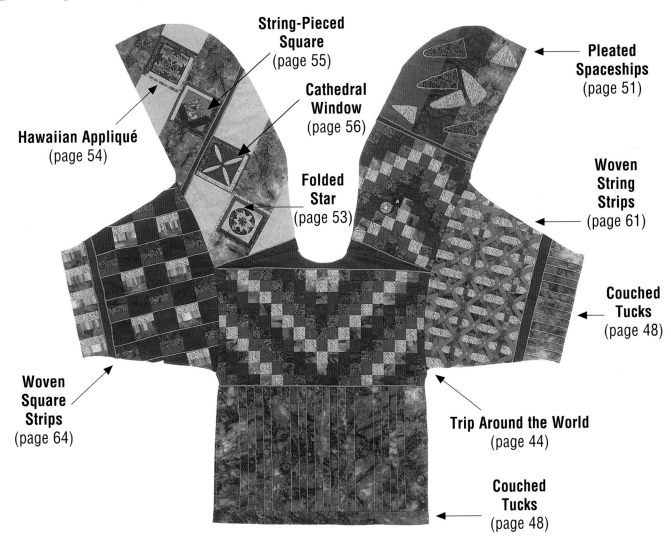

String-Pieced Square (page 55)

Cathedral Window (page 56)

Pleated Spaceships (page 51)

Hawaiian Appliqué (page 54)

Folded Star (page 53)

Woven String Strips (page 61)

Woven Square Strips (page 64)

Couched Tucks (page 48)

Trip Around the World (page 44)

Couched Tucks (page 48)

Mystery Jacket I (Long Version) by Bonnie Miller.

PREPARATION

1. Use the jacket pattern pieces for Jacket Five from the pullout section of *Jacket Jazz,* or substitute a commercially available pattern of a similar cardigan style. Decide which of the two jacket lengths—long or short—you prefer. Trace the pattern pieces onto pattern tissue or pattern tracing cloth and cut out. Adjust the finished length if necessary.

2. Cut the jacket fronts, back, and sleeves from the muslin or flannel foundation fabric. It is important to note that the sleeves in this jacket are finished with bias binding and require no seam allowance at the bottom edge. To make sure that the sleeve will be the correct finished length *before* you add the patchwork pieces to the sleeve foundation, pin the jacket front, back, and sleeve pieces together along the

½" seam lines and try on. Be sure to tuck the shoulder pad in place since it will raise the jacket on your shoulders and thereby shorten the sleeve. Adjust the sleeve length if needed.

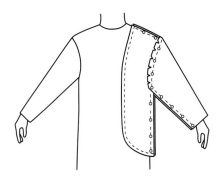

3. Working with each foundation piece separately, fuse 3"-wide strips of lightweight fusible interfacing to the wrong side of the front, neckline, and bottom edges. To make straight strips fit around curved edges, slash and spread or make tiny wedge-shaped cutouts in the interfacing as you position and fuse it in place.

4. Make and attach the patchwork pieces to each foundation, following the directions on pages 44–64.

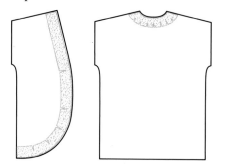

Shopping List

All yardage requirements are based on 44"-wide fabrics, unless otherwise noted. When using the same fabric for more than one patchwork technique, combine yardage requirements.

Yardage requirements for the jacket foundation and lining are given in a range to accommodate petite to extra-large sizes. If you are petite, buy the minimum yardage given. For large and extra-large sizes, buy the maximum. For sizes in the middle, split the difference.

Jacket Foundation	2½ to 3 yds. cotton flannel or muslin
Jacket Lining	2½ to 3 yds. silky lining or smooth cotton fabric
Interfacing	3/8 yd. lightweight fusible interfacing
Shoulder Pads	Raglan-style shoulder pads (3/8" to 3/4" thick)
Trip Around the World	¼ yd. each of 6 different fabrics and 1 contrasting fabric
	Fabric #1: Light
	Fabric #2: Medium
	Fabric #3: Dark
	Fabric #4: Light
	Fabric #5: Medium
	Fabric #6: Dark
	Fabric #8: This fabric should contrast with but help to unify the other fabrics.
Couched Tucks	1/3 yd. Fabric #7: accent for short version
	1¼ yds. Fabric #7: accent for long version. There will be a strip of fabric left over, approximately 18" x 36".

Pleated Spaceships	12" x 18" strip of Fabric #2 for pleats in short version
	¼ yd. Fabric #7 for short version
	12" x 18" piece each of Fabrics #4 and #5 for pleats in long version
	¼ yd. each of Fabrics #1, #2, and #7 for lower front of long version
	1" x 42" strip of Fabric #8 to divide lower portion of either version
Mystery Jazz Squares	¼ yd. each of Fabrics #3 and #4 for connectors, plus the fabrics listed below for each of the 4 blocks and Log Cabin borders
Folded Star Block	¼ yd. each of Fabrics #1 and #7
	2½" x 42" strip each of Fabrics #2, #3, and #6
Hawaiian Appliqué Block	4½" square of Fabric #3 for background
	3¾" square of Fabric #4 for appliqué
	4" square of Fine Fuse or Wonder-Under
String-Pieced	1½" x 12" strip each of Fabrics #1, #3, #4, and #6
Square Block	6" square of muslin or other lightweight fabric for foundation
Cathedral Window Block	10" square of Fabric #1 or #5
	4½" square of Fabric #1 or #5
Log Cabin Borders for	
Mystery Jazz Squares	1" x 42" strips each of 2 dark and 2 light fabrics (try Fabrics #5, #6, #7, and #8)
Yo-yos	Circles of fabric left over from Folded Star
Woven String Strips	6" x 42" strips each of Fabrics #1 and #6
	3" x 42" strip each of Fabrics #5 and #8
	9" x 42" strip of Fabric #2
	Leftover piece from Couched Tucks
Woven Square Strips	1½" x 42" strip each of Fabrics #1, #2, #3, #4, #5, and #6
	7" x 42" strip of Fabric #7
	3" x 42" strip of Fabric #8
Accent Trim	20 yds. round ribbon, soutache braid, cloisonné, fancy crochet thread, lightweight cording, rattail, or other trim not wider than ¼" that can be couched in place with a zigzag stitch
	Thread to match trim
Decorative Beads	I used a package of gold bugle beads on the long jacket; for the short jacket, I broke up an inexpensive bracelet of small, round wooden beads.

In addition to the fabrics and notions listed, you will need these special supplies:
Knife Pleater (EZE PLEATER or Perfect Pleater)
Bias bars in ½" or slightly narrower width

FABRIC SELECTION TIPS

- You will need eight different fabrics for this jacket.
- Choose two color families, including one light fabric, one medium fabric, and one dark fabric for each family. *A definite contrast between the lightest and darkest fabric is important.*
- Assign a number to each fabric, with Color #1 being the lightest in one family and Color #6 being the darkest in the other. The remaining two fabrics, #7 and #8, can be medium shades or may fit into a gradation of value from the lightest to darkest fabric.
- To avoid confusion later, make a swatch card to identify your fabrics. Be sure you have at least the total yardage listed below. In some cases, you may have more fabric than you actually need for the patchwork, but you can use it to make a patchwork lining.

Fabric #1	1 yd.
Fabric #2	1¼ yds.
Fabric #3	1 yd.
Fabric #4	1 yd.
Fabric #5	1 yd.
Fabric #6	½ yd.
Fabric #7	1¼ yds. Be sure this is an accent to the first six fabrics.
Fabric #8	⅝ yd.*

* This should be a unifying fabric, but it should contrast with the other seven fabrics.

√Trip Around the World

(Upper Back and Upper Right Front)

Make the patchwork for the back first, then use the leftovers for the front.

MATERIALS

¼ yd. each of 6 different fabrics (Fabrics #1–#6)*
¼ yd. of Fabric #8

*Select and label them as described under "Fabric Selection Tips" on page 43.

DIRECTIONS FOR UPPER BACK

1. Fold each fabric in half with selvages matching and make a clean cut along one cut edge. From each fabric, cut a 9"-wide strip.

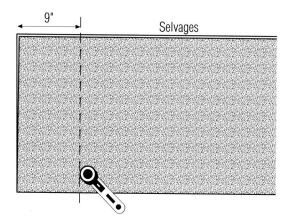

2. Open out the strips and layer them in 2 stacks of 3 strips each. Make sure the cut edges are lined up and all wrinkles are smoothed out. Trim away the selvages at one end of each stack, then crosscut 13 strips, each 2" x 9", from the layered strips. You should have a total of 78 strips. The strips are 1" longer than you actually need, to allow for trimming after you sew the sets together.

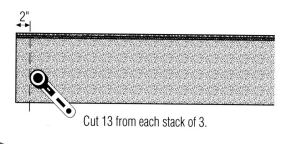

Cut 13 from each stack of 3.

Note: If one of your fabrics has a directional print that follows a horizontal line, cut 3 strips, each 2" wide, across the fabric width (crosswise grain). Cut a total of 12 strips, each 2" x 9", from the strips. Cut 1 more 2" x 9" strip from the remaining yardage. Repeat this cutting process for any fabric with a directional print.

Optional Cutting: For fabrics with an obvious horizontal design or pattern

3. Sort strips into 6 stacks, each containing identical fabrics. Number the strip stacks 1–6 to match the numbers in your shopping list.

4. Following the chart below, arrange strips into 8 sets (A–F) and identify each with the appropriate letter on a small piece of masking tape at the upper left-hand corner of the first strip in each set. (Set aside the remaining unused strips to use for fill-in squares when making the patchwork for the right front. You should have 1 strip each of Fabrics #3 and #6, and 2 strips each of Fabrics #4 and #5 left over.)

Using ¼"-wide seam allowances, sew the strips together in sets along the long cut edges. Press all seams in one direction, away from the strip with the masking-tape label. *Do not press over the masking tape.*

Check off each set as you complete it.

☐ Set A   #612345612   (Make 2 sets.)
☐ Set B   #123456123   (Make 2 sets.)
☐ Set C   #234561234   (Make 1 set.)
☐ Set D   #345612345   (Make 1 set.)
☐ Set E   #456123456   (Make 1 set.)
☐ Set F   #561234561   (Make 1 set.)

5. Stack the sets, right side up, in the order in which they were pieced. The top set should be Set F, and Fabric #5 should be the first (left-hand) strip. Make sure the strip sets are smooth and flat in the stack, with the long edges even and the top edges as even as possible. Place the stacked sets on a cutting board and make a clean cut at the end. Then cut the stacked

sets into 2"-wide strips. You will have a total of 32 pieced strips (4 groups of 8 patchwork strips in each).

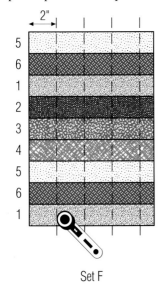

Set F

6. Following the illustration below, arrange the strips to create the design for the upper jacket back. You will need 2 complete groups of the patchwork strips and some of the strips from each of the remaining 2 groups. *Use the strips with the identifying masking-tape pieces last so you can have them to refer to if you get lost.*

Set B A F E D C B A B C D E F A B

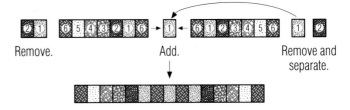

7. To prepare for sewing the strips together, begin at one side of the arranged strips and stack them in order. Put a safety pin in the top left corner of the first strip in the stack to remind you not to sew a strip to the left edge.

8. To sew, place the first strip with the pin in it, right side up, on the bed of the machine. Place the second strip on top of the first, right sides together. Stitch ¼" from the right-hand edge. As you sew over each pair of seam allowances, gently hold the strips so that the seam intersections match. There is no need to pin. Peek at each intersection as you approach it to make sure the seams match closely.

9. Continue adding strips in the same manner until you have completed the patchwork. Press all the seams in one direction, being careful not to distort the completed piece by using too much steam and/or tugging on it while pressing.

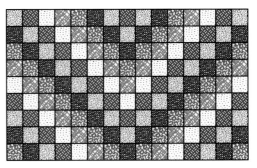

Completed Patchwork

Note: You have completed what could be the bottom half of a Trip Around the World crib or wall quilt. If you wish to make an entire quilt, repeat the above steps, then join the two pieces of patchwork at the center to complete the quilt top.

10. Remove squares #1 and #2 from the end of each of 2 remaining A strip sets. Sew the 2 strips together, with a #1 square between them.

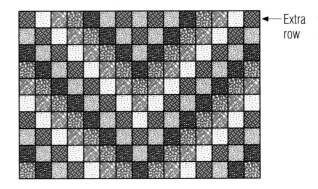

11. Sew the resulting strip to the top edge of the patchwork piece, matching the seam intersections carefully. Your patchwork should now have 10 squares down and 15 squares across. Press the seam in one direction.

12. Center the patchwork on the jacket back foundation, with the center square just below the back neck edge. Some of the foundation will show above the neckline and along the sides. A large section of the back foundation will be exposed below the patchwork.

Using pieced strips from the 2 remaining stacks, arrange strips as needed along the sides of the patchwork until it is large enough to cover the foundation all the way across. Since these strip sets have only 9 squares each, you will need to add squares to the top of each extra strip to continue the pattern. Cut 2" squares from leftover fabric strips and sew to the top edge. The foundation will still show below and slightly above the patchwork.

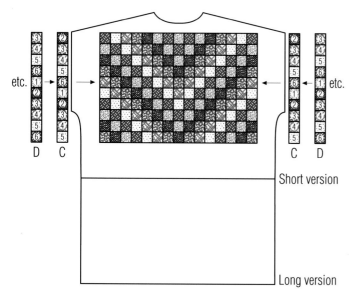

13. Pin the patchwork in place on the foundation. Turn the foundation over and stitch ⅛" from the side and armhole edges. Trim the patchwork even with the foundation where necessary.

14. Cut a strip of Fabric #8 that is 1" to 1½" wider than the widest area of exposed foundation above the patchwork, and 1" to 1½" longer than the top edge of the patchwork. Place the strip face down on the patchwork, aligning the raw edge with the upper raw edge of the patchwork. Stitch ¼" from the raw edges. Flip the fabric strip up over the exposed foundation and press. Pin to the foundation. Turn the piece over and trim the fabric even with the foundation edges. Stitch ⅛" from the shoulder and neckline edges.

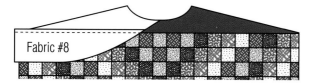

DIRECTIONS FOR UPPER RIGHT FRONT

1. Place the leftover strips from the back on a flat surface with all seams pressed toward you. Separate the strips into sets of matching strips. For example, when I made the jacket in the photo on pages 38 and 39, I had 3 strips of Set A, 4 strips of Set B, 2 of Set E, and 1 of Set F left over. The size of the jacket you are making and how you used the strips for the patchwork on the back determine the strips that are left over and how you will use them to make the patchwork on the front. Do not be alarmed if your leftovers do not match mine. For illustration purposes, the following steps are based on how I used my leftovers for my jacket.

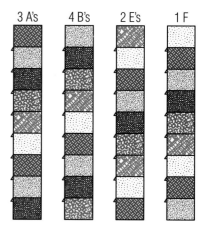

Your leftovers may differ slightly from mine.

2. Arrange the leftover strips in a symmetrical stair-step pattern similar to the jacket back. (It won't be identical.) Use a strip for the center and then do not repeat this strip in the remaining patchwork. I started with F in the center, then added an A strip to each side, then a B strip to each side. Your patchwork may look different than mine, depending on your leftovers.

Your strip set sequence may differ from this one.

3. For the next set of strips, I removed and discarded square #1 from each of the 2 remaining B strips. Then I added a 2" square of Fabric #4 to the bottom of each B strip.

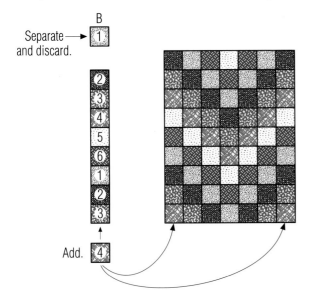

Separate and discard. B

Add. 4

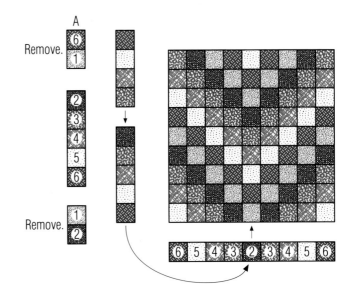

A

Remove.

Remove.

4. For the next set of strips, I removed and discarded square #6 from the bottom end of each of the 2 E strips and added a 2" square of Fabric #3 to the top of each one.

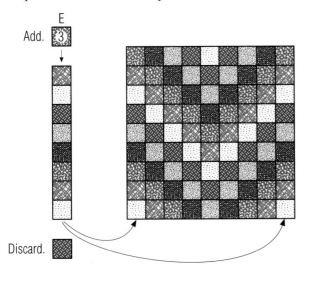

E

Add. 3

Discard.

5. To complete the patchwork, I used the remaining A strip and adjusted it so I could add it to the bottom edge of the patchwork. I removed square #1 and #2 from the bottom of the strip, and #1 and #6 from the top. Then I added 2" squares of Fabrics #3–#6 to the top.

6. After you have arranged and adjusted the patchwork strips for the front, stack and sew them together as described in steps 7–9 for the jacket back.

7. Draw a line on the upper right front foundation, making it the same length and angle as the top edge of the patchwork on one-half of the jacket back. *Do the same thing on the left front foundation so that the lines are positioned the same on both fronts for a uniform look.* Place the top edge of the completed patchwork along this line. If the patchwork is not wide enough to cover the foundation all the way to the armhole edge and side seam, add a strip of one of the busiest fabrics from your group of 6 fabrics to the armhole edge of the patchwork. Cut the strip 1" wider than the widest area of the foundation to be covered and add it to the patchwork. Pin the completed patchwork in place on the foundation. Trim outer edges even with foundation and stitch ⅛" from the raw edges.

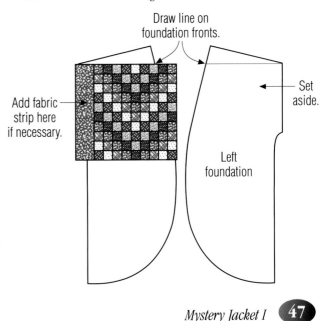

Draw line on foundation fronts.

Add fabric strip here if necessary.

Set aside.

Left foundation

8. Add a strip of Fabric #8 to the top edge to cover the foundation in the same manner as you did on the back. Flip onto the foundation, pin in place, then stitch through all layers ¹/₈" from the shoulder edge.

9. Measure the distance from the bottom edge of the patchwork to the bottom edge of the foundation at several locations. If the distance is not the same all the way across, pin or mark with chalk the same distance all the way across the bottom section of the patchwork. *If you are making the short version of this jacket, draw a line on the left front foundation the same distance from the bottom all the way across.*

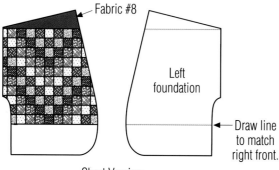

Short Version

10. Cut a 1"-wide strip of Fabric #8 as long as the bottom edge of the patchwork. With right sides together, position the strip on top of the patchwork so that the raw edge is even with the bottom edge of the patchwork if the distance is the same all the way across. If it is not, match the strip to the raw edge of the patchwork and then shift it onto the patchwork as needed so that the strip is parallel to the bottom edge of the jacket. Stitch the strip in place ¹/₄" from the strip's raw edge. Flip onto the foundation and press.

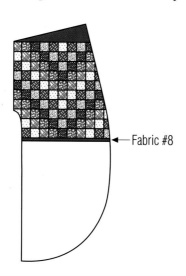

✓Couched Tucks

(Lower Jacket Back)

MATERIALS

¹/₃ yd. accent fabric (Fabric #7) for short version or 1¹/₄ yds. for long version*
Approximately 3¹/₂ yds. trim or decorative yarn
Thread to match or coordinate with fabric and trim

*There will be a leftover strip, approximately 18" x 36".

DIRECTIONS FOR SHORT VERSION

1. Unfold Fabric #7 and place wrong side up on the ironing board. Measure in 4" from the raw edge at both ends and snip mark. Fold fabric onto itself, wrong sides together, at the snips. Measure to make sure that you have turned back exactly 4" all along, then press from selvage to selvage along the fold. Pin in place. Thread the machine with matching thread and stitch 1" from the pressed edge. Remove the pins.

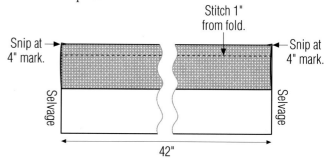

2. With the right side of the fabric against the ironing board, press the stitched tuck toward the untucked end.

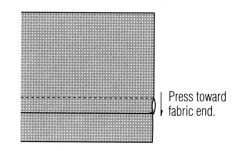

3. Measure and snip the selvages 2" from the stitching. Fold at the snips, then measure to make sure the fold is 2" from the stitching along the entire length. Press. Stitch 1" from the fold and press the tuck in the same direction as the first.

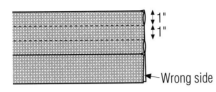

↕1"
↕1"

←Wrong side

4. Repeat step 3 to make a third and final tuck.

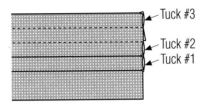

←Tuck #3

←Tuck #2
←Tuck #1

5. Measure the distance from the bottom of Fabric #8 to the bottom edge of the foundation and add ½". Cut a strip this width from the tucked strip.

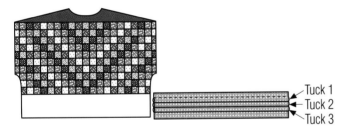

←Tuck 1
←Tuck 2
←Tuck 3

6. To couch trim to the edge of each tuck: Thread the machine with matching thread. Set it for a zigzag stitch so the stitches are about ¼" apart (stitch length) and wide enough to catch the edge of the tuck and clear the edge of the decorative cord. The stitch setting will vary, depending on the width of the trim you are using, so it is important to test the stitch settings and practice first on scraps. Refer to the illustration with step 7 above right.

Note: To keep trim from tangling or rolling away, place trim in a bag and tape the bag to the edge of your sewing-machine table. Pull the trim from the bag as you stitch.

7. Place the first tuck on the bed of the sewing machine under the presser foot, with the remaining fabric to the left of the needle. Arrange the trim snugly against the folded edge of the tuck, with at least 1" of the trim extending behind the presser foot. (If you have a cording foot for your machine, you can try it for this technique as it will leave your hands freer to guide the fabric.) While holding the trim taut in front of the needle, zigzag the trim in place next to the fold.

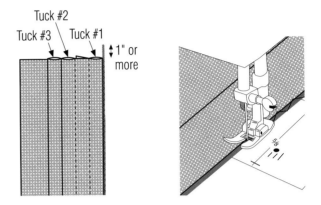

Tuck #2
Tuck #3   Tuck #1

↕1" or more

8. Couch the remaining tucks in the same manner, being careful to keep the other tucks and fabric out of the way of the stitching.

9. Place the completed couched and tucked strip right side down, aligning the upper raw edge with the bottom raw edge of the patchwork, and one short end with the right-hand edge of the jacket foundation. The excess fabric will extend beyond the left-hand edge of the foundation. Stitch ¼" from the long edge through all layers. Flip the tucked strip down on top of the foundation; press and pin in place. Turn the jacket back over and trim the tucked strip even with the side and bottom edges of the foundation. Stitch ⅛" from the raw edges. Save leftover pieces for the Woven String Strips on pages 61–63.

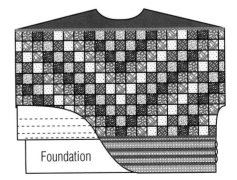

Foundation

10. Place a piece of trim in the ditch of the seam where the tucked strip joins the patchwork and at the upper edge where Fabric #8 meets the patchwork. Couch in place. Position a piece of cord on top of the visible stitching line, just below the seam line, and couch in place.

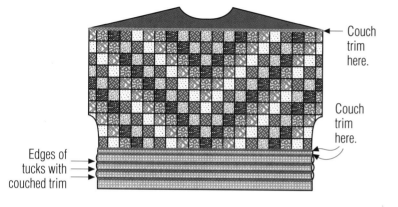

Couch trim here.

Couch trim here.

Edges of tucks with couched trim

DIRECTIONS FOR LONG VERSION

1. Measure the amount of foundation showing below the patchwork in the upper jacket back and add 1". This measurement will be around 18". Cut a piece of Fabric #7 this width, cutting along the fabric length as shown. Set the remaining fabric aside for other patchwork.

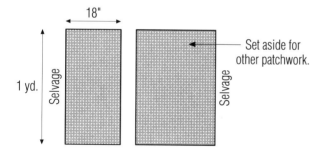

18"

1 yd.

Selvage

Selvage

Set aside for other patchwork.

2. Place the strip on the ironing board, wrong side up, with the short end parallel to the length of the board. Follow steps 1–4 for the short version, making tucks parallel to the short end of the strip.

3. Next, measure 4½" from last stitching line and repeat steps 1–4 for the short version.

4. Repeat step 3 as many times as needed to create a tucked strip that will cover the width of the lower foundation. The finished tucks will be vertical.

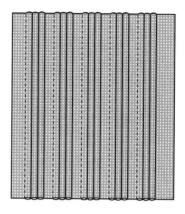

5. Couch trim to the folded edges of each tuck as described in steps 6–8 for the short version.

6. Place the tucked panel on top of the patchwork with right sides together and raw edges even. Stitch ¼" from the raw edges. Flip the tucked strip down on top of the foundation and press. Pin in place. Turn the jacket over and trim the strip even with the edges of the foundation. Stitch ⅛" from the raw edges. Save leftover pieces for the right sleeve (pages 61–63).

7. Couch trim in place at the upper and lower seam lines of the completed patchwork and along the first exposed seam of each series of tucks as described in step 10 for the short version.

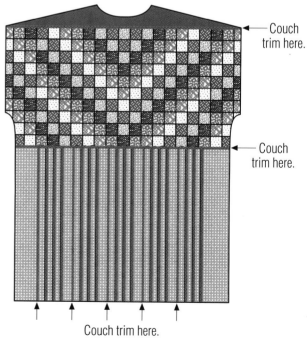

Couch trim here.

Couch trim here.

Couch trim here.

√Pleated Spaceships

(Lower Right Front)

MATERIALS

Short Version	Long Version
¼ yd. of Fabric #7 for lower front	¼ yd. each of Fabrics #1, #2, and #7 for lower front
12" x 18" piece of Fabric #2 for pleats	12" x 18" piece each of Fabrics #4 and #5 for pleats
1"-wide strip of Fabric #8	1"-wide strip of Fabric #8
Scraps of fusible interfacing	Scraps of fusible interfacing
Approximately 1 yd. trim	Approximately 1 yd. trim
Template plastic	Template plastic

You will need the Perfect Pleater or EZE PLEATER, designed to make ¼"-deep tucks. These tools have stiff, permanent tucks, which are called "louvers."

DIRECTIONS

Use the templates on page 69 for the spaceship shapes.

1. For the *short version*, cut a rectangle of Fabric #7 large enough to cover the foundation still exposed below Trip Around the World on the right front, *plus ½" extra all around.* The Pleated Spaceships will peek through this fabric. Set aside.

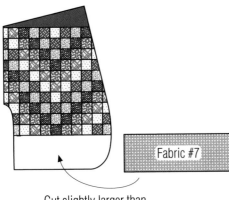

Cut slightly larger than exposed foundation.

For the *long version*, measure the width of the foundation showing below the patchwork and divide it into 3 equal widths. For example, if the patchwork measures 12" across, each of the 3 sections will measure 4" wide. To this measurement, add ½" for seam allowances. Cut a strip this width from Fabrics #1, #2, and #7.

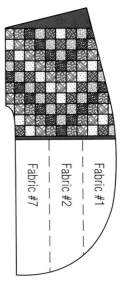

Divide into thirds.

Arrange the 3 strips so Fabric #7 strip will be closest to the side seam. Sew strips together, using ¼"-wide seam allowances; press the seams to one side. The Pleated Spaceships will peek through this multi-fabric piece. Set aside.

2. To make the spaceships, use the pleater board and the 12" x 18" pieces of fabric. Each piece will yield a 6" x 12" piece of knife-pleated fabric. Place the pleater board on the ironing board with the louvered edges away from you. Position one of the 12" x 18" pieces of fabric *wrong side up* with the 12" edge ready to go in the first louver of the pleater board.

3. Firmly tuck the fabric into the louver closest to you, using a very thin metal or plastic ruler or a credit card for best results. Repeat this process, tucking fabric firmly into every louver until you have pleated the entire 18" length of fabric.

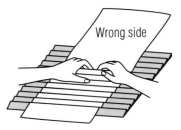

4. Set the iron on cotton (unless you are using a more delicate fabric) and steam press the pleats while the fabric is still in the louvers.

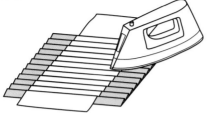

5. Cut a strip of fusible interfacing the size of the tucked piece. Place the fusible side against the wrong side of the tucked piece and fuse in place. The interfacing will hold the pleats permanently in place, so be sure to follow the manufacturer's directions for fusing, using adequate steam and pressure. *Allow to cool*.

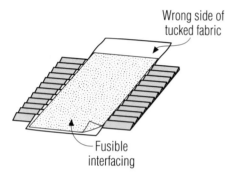

Wrong side of tucked fabric

Fusible interfacing

6. To remove the pleated fabric, roll the pleater away from it.
7. Decide how many and which spaceship shapes on page 69 you want to use. I suggest 2 to 3 ships for the short jacket and 5 to 6 for the long jacket. Trace the desired shapes onto template plastic and cut out.
8. Arrange the template shapes on the right side of the fabric you set aside for the lower right front. When happy with the arrangement, draw around each shape with a sharp pencil.

Short Version

Draw around template shapes.

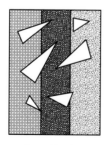

Long Version

Cut out each shape, staying ¼" *inside* the drawn lines. Clip almost to the drawn line at each corner of each spaceship shape.

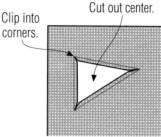

Clip into corners.

Cut out center.

9. Turn under the raw edge along the drawn line and press. Arrange a piece of pleated fabric behind the prepared opening and pin in place. Stitch close to the folded edges through all layers. Turn the piece over and trim away the excess pleated fabric close to the stitching. Repeat to complete each of the remaining Pleated Spaceships.

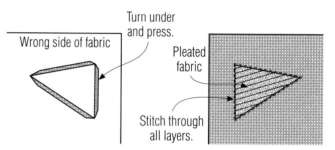

Wrong side of fabric

Turn under and press.

Pleated fabric

Stitch through all layers.

10. Place the Pleated Spaceships piece on top of the fabric strip at the lower edge of the Trip Around the World patchwork, with right sides together and raw edges even. Stitch ¼" from the raw edges. Flip the Pleated Spaceships down on top of the foundation; press and pin in place. Turn the right front over and trim the piece even with the edges of the foundation. Stitch ⅛" from the raw edges.

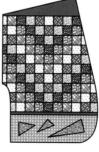

Short Version

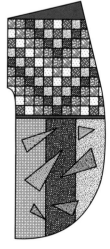

Long Version

11. Set up your machine for couching as described in step 6 for Couched Tucks on page 49. Couch trim in the ditch of both seams of the strip at the bottom edge of the patchwork as shown for the jacket back in step 10 on page 50. Repeat at the seam where Fabric #8 meets the top edge of the patchwork.

Couch trim around the inner edge of each spaceship. To hide the tails of the trim, thread them into a tapestry needle and insert the blunt point of the needle under the edge between the stitches. Bring the point through the foundation fabric and tie the ends off in a overhand knot.

✓Mystery Jazz Squares

(Left Front)

Folded Star Block

MATERIALS

¼ yd. each of Fabrics #1 and #7
2½" x 42" strip each of Fabrics #2, #3, and #6

DIRECTIONS

Use the circle template on page 69.
1. Cut 4 squares, each 2" x 2", from Fabric #1 for the center of the square. Cut a 5" square from the same fabric.
2. Fold the 5" square corner to corner diagonally, then in half again. Press to mark the square with an X. Unfold.

3. Cut 8 squares, each 2" x 2", from each of Fabrics #2, #3, and #6. You will have a total of 24 squares.
4. Fold each of the 2" squares of Fabric #1 in half with wrong sides together and press. Fold corners C and D to the center to make a triangle. Press. Repeat with squares of Fabrics #2,

#3, and #6. Each group of squares will make 1 round of points on the star.

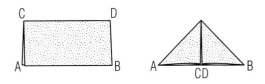

5. Decide the order in which you want to use the 3 outer fabrics. The star shows up best when rows are arranged in contrasting values of light and dark.
6. Position the 4 center triangles on the creased 5" square so the points meet in the center and line up with the creases. Pin in place. Tack the points in place at the center with almost invisible stitches between the folds. Machine stitch the outer raw edges of the triangles through all layers. This makes the center of the star.

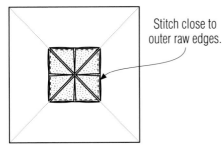

Stitch close to outer raw edges.

Tack in center.

7. Arrange the 8 triangles of the next color with their points ¼" from the center and directly in line with the points of the first 4 triangles. Position the triangles in a clockwise fashion so the raw edges overlap in a consistent direction. Tack the tips in place as invisibly as possible and machine stitch the raw edges through all layers.

Arrange, tack, and stitch the triangles for the remaining 2 rounds of star points in the same manner. When the star is complete, you will have an octagon shape on the background square.

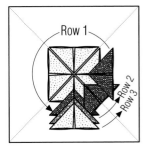

Triangles form an octagon.

8. Trace the circle on page 69 onto template plastic and place the template on top of the completed star. Make sure the raw edges of the outer round of star points extend at least $\frac{1}{4}$" beyond the outer edge of the template. If not, adjust the template size as needed.

9. Cut two 5" squares from Fabric #7 or another fabric that contrasts well with the outer row of star points.

10. Center the circle template on the wrong side of one of the 5" squares and draw around it. Place the 2 squares right sides together with all raw edges even. Stitch around the circle through both layers.

11. Carefully cut out the circle center through both layers, leaving a $\frac{1}{4}$"-wide seam allowance all around. Clip the seam allowance to the stitching, spacing clips every 2" around the circle. Set the circles aside to use for 2 Yo-yos on the right front. (See page 61.)

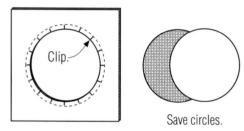

Save circles.

12. Turn the piece right side out and press along the seam edge. Center the folded star behind the opening in the square. Lift the upper square away and pin the lower square to the star. Stitch close to the first stitching to attach the window to the star. No stitching will show on the right side.

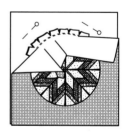

13. Press the completed star, then trim the square to $4\frac{1}{2}$" x $4\frac{1}{2}$", making sure the star is centered. Stitch raw edges together with a scant $\frac{1}{4}$"-wide seam allowance. Set aside for the left front.

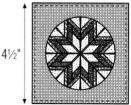

Stitch $\frac{1}{4}$" from edges.

Hawaiian Appliqué Block

MATERIALS

$4\frac{1}{2}$" square of Fabric #3 for background
$3\frac{3}{4}$" square of Fabric #4 for appliqué
4" square of Fine Fuse or Wonder-Under
$3\frac{3}{4}$" square of paper

DIRECTIONS

1. Fold the paper square in half with all edges even. Crease firmly. Fold in half again and crease. *Make sure that the folding is exact and all edges are even.* Fold in half again to create a folded triangle.

2. Create a snowflake drawing on the folded paper or use the design below. *Make sure that the shape is arranged so that you will not be cutting along the folded edge.* Cut out and decide if you are happy with the design. If not, repeat with a different shape. When you are happy with the design, cut a $\frac{1}{8}$ section from the paper snowflake and mark the places where it touches a fold. This is your appliqué pattern.

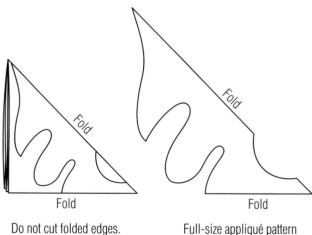

Do not cut folded edges.   Full-size appliqué pattern

3. Following the manufacturer's directions, apply Fine Fuse or Wonder-Under to the wrong side of the appliqué fabric square. If using Wonder-Under, remove the paper now.

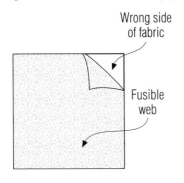

Wrong side of fabric

Fusible web

4. Fold the appliqué fabric square in the same sequence as you did the paper square, with wrong sides together. *Use your fingers to crease each fold before making the next one.* Place your paper pattern on the folded fabric, pin in place, and cut through all 8 layers at once.

5. Open the folded fabric shape and center it, right side up, on the right side of the background fabric square. Make sure the snowflake points are aimed at the outer corners of the background square. Pin in place, starting at the center and working out toward the edges. The snowflake should be symmetrical with equal space all around.

6. When you are satisfied with the placement, carefully remove the pins and fuse in place, following the manufacturer's directions. Use your favorite machine-appliqué stitch to embellish the outer edges. I used a machine blanket stitch.

String-Pieced Square Block

Materials

1½" x 12" strips each of Fabrics #1, #3, #4, and #6
6" square of muslin or other lightweight fabric

Directions

1. Fold the muslin square in half on the diagonal. Press, then open out and draw a line ¼" above the crease. Place the Fabric #1 strip with one raw edge along the drawn line. Pin in place. Cut away the part of the strip that extends beyond the edges of the square.

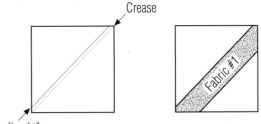

Crease

Draw line ¼" above crease.

Fabric #1

2. Place the Fabric #4 strip face down, aligning one raw edge with the upper edge of Strip #1. Pin, then stitch through all layers ¼" from the raw edges. *This seam should run from corner to corner of the muslin square beneath.* Flip the strip onto the foundation; press carefully, pin in place, and trim.

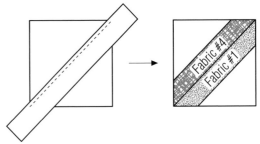

Fabric #4
Fabric #1

3. Referring to the illustration for placement, continue adding strips in the same manner until you have used each of the strips 2 times to cover the muslin square. Turn the square to the muslin side and stitch ⅛" from the raw edges. Press.

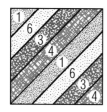

4. Cut the square into 4 equal squares, each approximately 3" square. Lay the squares on a flat surface and rotate so the seam lines form a square in the center. Sew the squares together in rows, then sew the rows together to make a 4½" pieced square. Trim if necessary. Press.

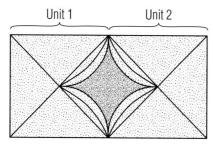

Row 1
Row 2

Cathedral Window Block

Many quiltmakers are familiar with the stitched and folded Cathedral Window unit. This variation, called "Secret Garden" in Lynne Edward's book *Through the Window & Beyond*, can be done one square at a time.

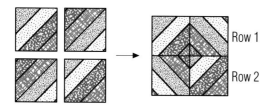

Unit 1   Unit 2

Traditional Cathedral Window requires 2 units.

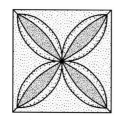

Secret Garden
Single Unit

MATERIALS

10" square of Fabric #1 or #5*
4½" square of Fabric #1 or #5*
*The 4½" square must contrast with the 10" square. If #1 and #5 in your selection of fabrics do not contrast, select two that do.

DIRECTIONS

1. Fold the 10" square into a rectangle with right sides together. Stitch ¼" from the raw edges at each short end.

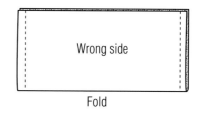

Wrong side

Fold

2. Pull the rectangle open and bring the sides together, keeping raw edges even and seams matching. Stitch, leaving a 2"-wide opening in the center for turning.

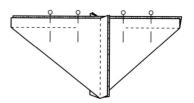

3. Clip the corners to eliminate bulk and press the seams open, being careful not to press creases in the outer edges.

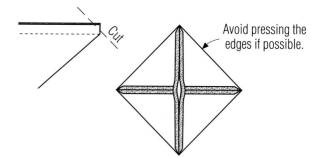

Cut

Avoid pressing the edges if possible.

4. Turn the piece right side out through the opening and press. There is no need to complete the 2" seam that was left open, since it will be permanently covered. Place the $4\frac{1}{2}$" square of contrasting fabric on-point on the seamed side of the square and hand baste in place close to the raw edges.

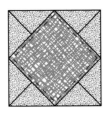

5. Fold the points of the square to the center over the small square and connect the points with hidden stitches.

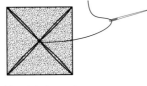

Fold points to center;
tack in place.

6. Roll the edge of each triangle back to reveal the square below and slipstitch in place, ending $\frac{1}{2}$" from the outer corners. Slipstitch the corner edges together.

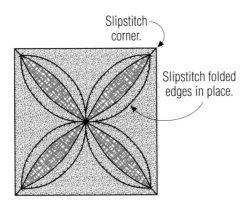

Slipstitch corner.

Slipstitch folded edges in place.

Log Cabin Borders

Add a Log Cabin border to the Folded Star, Hawaiian Appliqué, String-Pieced Square, and Cathedral Window blocks.

MATERIALS

Folded Star, Hawaiian Appliqué, String-Pieced Square, and Cathedral Window blocks
1"x 42" strip each of 2 dark and 2 light fabrics (try Fabrics #5, #6, #7, and #8)

DIRECTIONS

1. With right sides together and using $\frac{1}{4}$"-wide seams, sew a dark strip to one side of each of the 4 blocks. Finger-press the strip away from the block edge. Turn each block counter-clockwise and, using the same strip of dark fabric, sew the strip to the second side. Finger-press away from the block center.

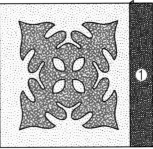

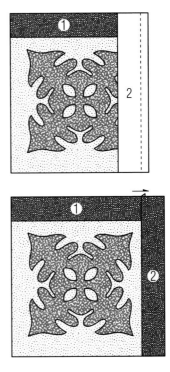

2. Using a light fabric strip, add strips to the remaining edges of each block in the same manner. Press each block with the iron.

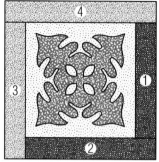

3. Repeat steps 1 and 2, using the remaining 2 strips of fabric: 1 light and 1 dark. Each block should now have a dark half and a light half.

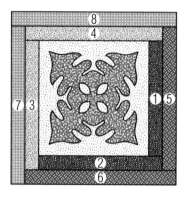

Finishing the Left Front

(Long Version)

MATERIALS

4 Log Cabin bordered blocks
2 leftover fabrics for connectors*
1" x 42" strip and a small scrap of Fabric #8 for upper
  shoulder
Couching trim
Beads

    *Choose fabrics you did not use for the Log Cabin borders. Fabrics #3 and #4 are referenced in the directions, but you may use others if you prefer.

DIRECTIONS

1. Measure the completed blocks to make sure they are all 6½" square. If they are not, trim them all to the same size.
2. Place the left front foundation right side up on a flat surface.
3. Referring to the illustration, decide how you want to arrange the blocks on the jacket front. Position them in their approximate locations on the foundation, below the shoulder line you marked on the foundation (step 7 for the right front on page 47). Place them so that the Log Cabin borders that touch each other are the same fabric (dark or light).

Arrange blocks
on left front.

4. Cut a strip equal to the width of the blocks from each of the connector fabrics.
5. Sew a piece of Fabric #3 to opposite sides of the first block. Press the seams toward Fabric #3.

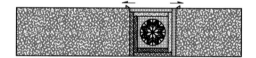

    Pin the block strip in place on the foundation so it is centered between the center front and arm-hole edges, and the top point is at the drawn line. Trim the excess connector fabric at each edge of the foundation and ¼" *above the drawn line at the top.*

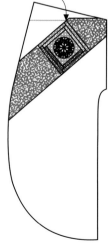

Point of square
at drawn line

Place block equal
distance from
right and left.

6. With right sides together and raw edges even, stitch a strip of Fabric #4 to the top edge of the block strip. Flip onto the foundation; press and pin in place. Trim even with the foundation front edge and with ¼" extending above the drawn line.

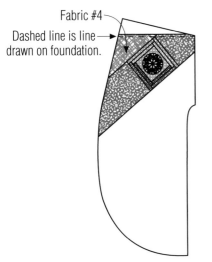

Fabric #4

Dashed line is line drawn on foundation.

7. In the same manner, add a strip of Fabric #8 at the drawn line and trim all edges even with the foundation. Stitch ⅛" from the outer raw edges.

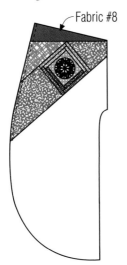

Fabric #8

8. Add strips of Fabric #4 to the right and left sides of the second block. Press the seams toward Fabric #4. Place the block strip on top of the first block strip with raw edges even, making sure the block points are centered between the front and armhole edges. Stitch ¼" from the raw edges. Flip down onto the foundation; press, pin in place, and trim edges even with the foundation. Refer to the illustration following step 10 below.

9. If your jacket is long enough, use the stitch-and-flip method to add a Fabric #8 strip (½" finished width) at the bottom of the second strip. (Make sure that all of the bottom block will fit before you do this. See note below.)

Note: In the jacket pictured on page 38, I did not have enough space on the foundation to add the strip with the stitch-and-flip method. Instead, I completed the block placement, then appliquéd a finished ½"-wide strip on top of the completed patchwork. This strip covered some of the Log Cabin border on the two adjoining blocks.

10. Make block strips using the remaining blocks and alternating Fabrics #3 and #4. Add to the foundation in the manner described above. Trim all excess even with the foundation, then stitch ⅛" from the raw edges. Cover any exposed foundation below the block strip with the next fabric in your rotation (Fabric #3 or #4).

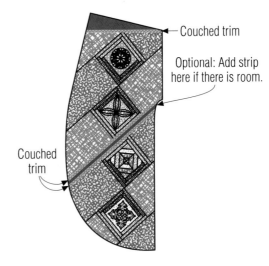

Couched trim

Optional: Add strip here if there is room.

Couched trim

11. Couch trim along the seam line at the bottom edge of Fabric #8 at the shoulder and along both edges of the strip between the second and third blocks. (See step 6 on page 49 for couching directions.)

12. Stitch beads where blocks touch at the Log Cabin borders. Refer to the jacket photo on page 38.

Finishing the Left Front

(Short Version)

Refer to the "Materials" list for "Finishing the Left Front" of the long version on page 58.

DIRECTIONS

1. Complete steps 1 and 2 as directed on page 58 for the long version.

2. Referring to the illustration below, decide how you want to arrange the blocks on the jacket front. Position them in their approximate locations on the foundation, below the shoulder line you marked on the foundation (step 7 for the right front on page 47). Place the blocks so the Log Cabin borders that touch each other are of the same fabric (dark or light).

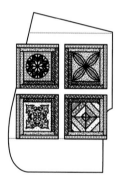

3. Stitch the blocks together in 2 rows, then stitch the rows together, taking care to match the center seams. Press.

4. Place the bottom edge of the completed patchwork piece ¼" below the lower line you drew on the left front foundation (step 9 for the right front on page 48). Center the patchwork on the foundation and pin in place. Machine stitch in-the-ditch of the center horizontal and vertical seams to anchor the patchwork to the foundation.

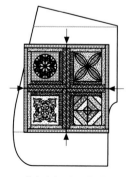

Stitch in-the-ditch.

5. Cover any exposed foundation at the center front and armhole edges, using the same fabric as the outermost Log Cabin border strip on the blocks. Use the stitch-and-flip method to sew the strips in place. Trim strips even with the foundation. *Refer to the illustration with step 9 for the following steps.*

6. Cut a 1"-wide strip of Fabric #8 the length of the bottom edge of the patchwork. Stitch in place using the stitch-and-flip method. Press and pin in place.

7. Cut strips of Fabrics #3 and #4, making them ½" wider than the exposed foundation below the strip of Fabric #8. Sew them together at the short end and press the seam to one side. Line up this seam with the center seam of the patchwork as you stitch and flip the piece onto the foundation. Trim even with the foundation edges and stitch ⅛" from the raw edges. Repeat at the top edges of the patchwork and trim excess away, allowing ¼" to extend above the drawn line.

8. Add a strip of Fabric #8 to cover the foundation above the patchwork, using the stitch-and-flip method. Trim edges even with the foundation; stitch ⅛" from all edges.

9. Couch trim along the seam lines of Fabric #8 at the shoulder and at the bottom. (See page 49.)

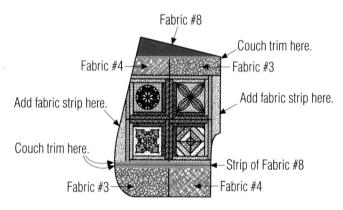

10. Stitch beads to the upper and lower sections on the patchwork (Fabrics #3 and #4), adding one bead at a time to create a zigzag design.

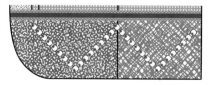

✓ Yo-yos

(Upper Right Front)

MATERIALS

2 circles saved from the Folded Star block
A few small beads

DIRECTIONS

1. Thread a needle with double thread and knot the ends together. Turn under 1/8" at the edge of the circle and do a running stitch very close to the folded edge. Draw up the thread as tightly as possible to form a tight circle and backstitch to secure. Repeat for the second Yo-yo.

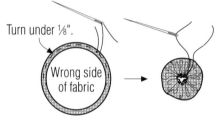

Turn under 1/8".

Wrong side of fabric

2. Arrange the Yo-yos, stitching side up, on the jacket front in the Trip Around the World patchwork where they will show best. Blindstitch or feather stitch around the outer edge of each Yo-yo to hold it in place. Add decorative beads to a section of each Yo-yo as shown.

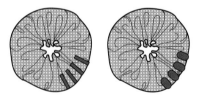

Add decorative beads.

✓ Woven String Strips

(Right Sleeve)

MATERIALS*

4 strips, each 1 1/2" x 42", of Fabric #1
4 strips, each 1 1/2" x 42", of Fabric #6
2 strips, each 1 1/2" x 42", of Fabric #5
6 strips, each 1 1/2" x 42", of Fabric #2
3" x 42" strip of Fabric #8
Leftover piece from Couched Tucks
Couching trim
Beads

*Fabrics must contrast so that the weaving pattern is visible.

DIRECTIONS

1. Fold the right sleeve foundation in half lengthwise and press along the fold. Set aside.
2. Cut each strip of Fabrics #1 and #6 into 3 pieces, each 14" long, for a total of 24 strips.
3. Choose the fabric on which markings will show the best on the wrong side, then mark each of these 12 strips as shown.

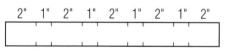

2" 1" 2" 1" 2" 1" 2" 1" 2"

Mark on wrong side of fabric.

4. Place each Fabric #1 strip face down on a Fabric #6 strip. With the marked strip of each pair face up, stitch ¼" from one set of raw edges in each pair, stitching only the 2"-long sections. To do this quickly, stop stitching at the mark, lift the presser foot, and pull enough thread to reach to the next mark. Lower the presser foot and continue stitching in the same manner. Clip excess thread between stitched sections. Press the seams open in each pair.

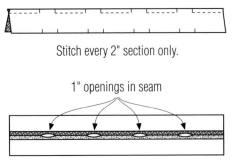

Stitch every 2" section only.

1" openings in seam

Press seam open.

5. Sew the pairs together to create a finished piece of patchwork. Press all seams open.

6. Cut each Fabric #5 strip in half to make 4 strips of equal length, each approximately 22" long. *With wrong sides together*, stitch ⅛" from the raw edges on each of the 4 strips to form fabric tubes.

7. Insert a ½"-wide bias bar into a strip and bring the seam to the center of the bar. Press the seam to one side. Repeat with the remaining strips.

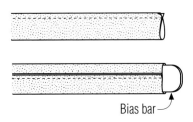

Bias bar

8. Starting at the top edge on the right side of the patchwork fabric, weave a strip in and out through the 1" openings in Row 1 of the patchwork. Begin weaving from the back of the patchwork for Row 2. Repeat the weaving pattern for the first 2 rows.

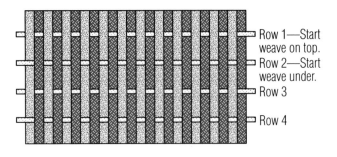

Row 1—Start weave on top.
Row 2—Start weave under.
Row 3
Row 4

9. Fold each strip of Fabric #2 in half lengthwise with wrong sides together and stitch ⅛" from the raw edges. Press as described in step 7. You will have to slide the bias bar along inside the tube as you work since it is not as long as your fabric tube.

10. Weave the finished strips of Fabric #2 diagonally under the strips of Fabric #5, beginning in the upper left corner and working diagonally from left to right. Trim excess fabric strip. Skip a #1 and #6 patchwork strip before starting to weave the second strip. Continue weaving with the strips until you have woven in 8 or 9 strips.

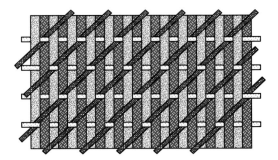

11. Now weave with the strips of Fabric #2 in the opposite diagonal direction, running the strips over the first strips of Fabric #2. The strips should create an X on the top of the patchwork fabric and go under a Fabric #5 strip where they cross.

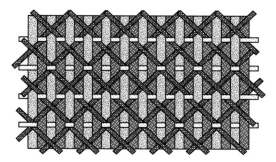

12. Locate the center of the completed piece and mark with a pin. Place the piece right side up on top of the right sleeve foundation, with the top edge at the top edge of the sleeve cap, and the patchwork centered on the foundation. Pin in place. Turn the piece over and stitch $1/8$" from the raw edges of the foundation at the underarms and around the sleeve cap. Trim even with the foundation, saving the scraps for another project.

13. Place the leftover Couched Tucks on top of the lower section of the sleeve to make sure it is long enough to cover the width of the foundation from underarm seam to underarm seam. Pin the Couched Tucks strip to the sleeve with one edge along the bottom edge of the sleeve. Stitch $1/8$" from the upper edge. Turn the sleeve over, stitch $1/8$" from the foundation edges, and trim even with the foundation.

Note: If you are making the long jacket, the tucks will be vertical as shown in the illustration below. If you are making the short jacket, the tucks will be horizontal.

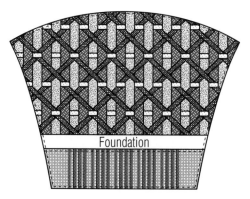

Add couched tucks to lower portion of sleeve.

14. Measure the exposed foundation and cut a Fabric #8 strip that is $1/2$" wider than the space and long enough to cover the sleeve. Turn under and press $1/4$" along one long edge. Using the stitch-and-flip method, stitch the strip to the bottom edge of the woven patchwork. Press, pin in place, and edgestitch along the turned edge.

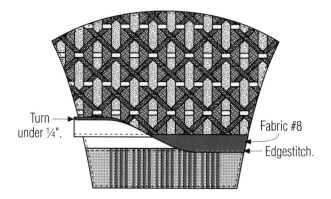

Turn under $1/4$".

Fabric #8

Edgestitch.

15. Couch accent trim along both edges of the Fabric #8 strip. (See step 10 on page 50 for couching directions.)

16. Sew a cluster of 3 beads in the center of each X formed where Fabric #2 strips cross.

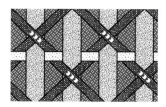

✓ *Woven Square Strips*

(Left Sleeve)

MATERIALS

1½" x 42" strip each of Fabrics #1, #2, #3, #4, #5, and #6*
2 strips, each 3½" x 42", of Fabric #7
3" x 42" strip of Fabric #8
Couching trim
*Piece these to the required length from fabric leftovers if necessary.

DIRECTIONS

1. Using ¼"-wide seams, sew the fabric strips together in sets of 3 to make Strip Unit A with Fabrics 1/2/3 and Strip Unit B with Fabrics 4/5/6. Sew them together so they go from light to dark in each set. Each strip-pieced unit should measure 3½" x 42". Crosscut each unit into 12 squares, each 3½" x 3½", for a total of 24 squares, 12A and 12B.

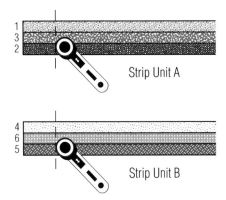

2. From the strips of Fabric #7, cut a total of 19 squares, each 3½" x 3½". These are the C squares in the illustration below. Arrange the squares on a flat surface in the order shown in the illustration. Set aside the 5 extra B squares for the bottom edge of the sleeve.

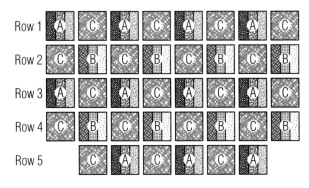

3. Using a ¼"-wide seam allowance, sew the squares together in rows. Press the seams in opposite directions from row to row. Sew the rows together, matching seam intersections .

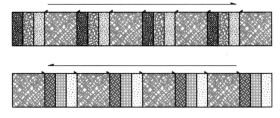

Press seams in opposite directions.

4. Fold the left sleeve foundation in half lengthwise and press the fold. Open the foundation and place face up on a flat surface. Center the completed patchwork on the foundation and pin in place. Turn the sleeve over and stitch ⅛" from the foundation edges. Trim even with the foundation. Couch accent trim vertically along the seam lines joining the squares. (See step 6 on page 49 for couching directions.)

5. Sew the remaining B squares together in a row. Place the long edge even with the bottom edge of the foundation. Pin in place.

6. Cut a strip of Fabric #8 wide enough to cover the exposed sleeve foundation, plus ½", and long enough to fit across the sleeve. Sew to the bottom edge of the patchwork using the stitch-and-flip method. Press and pin in place. Sew the row of B squares to the bottom edge of Fabric #8 in the same manner. Press, pin in place, then turn the sleeve over and stitch ⅛" from the raw edges of the foundation. Trim even with the foundation.

7. Couch accent trim along both edges of the Fabric #8 strip.

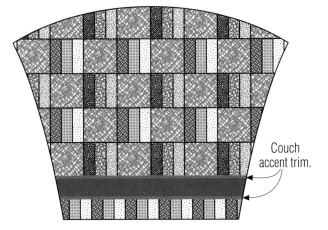

Couch accent trim.

✓Jacket Finishing

Use ½"-wide seam allowances.

1. Using ¼ yd. of Fabric #8, cut enough 3"-wide true bias strips to make a piece 3½ to 4 yds. long. Fold the strip in half lengthwise, wrong sides together; press.

2. Sew the jacket fronts to the back at the shoulder seam and press the seam open. If you wish, add couching or piping.

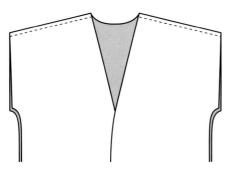

Stitch shoulder seams.

3. Sew the sleeves to the jacket armholes, matching shoulders and notches. Press the seam open. If you wish, you can couch or pipe this seam.

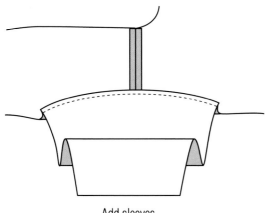

Add sleeves.

4. Cut and assemble the lining in the same manner. Place the completed jacket on top of the wrong side of the lining and trim lining to match jacket if necessary.

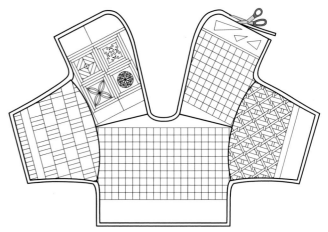

Note: I cut the lining pieces for my long jacket from the leftover patchwork pieces. Both sleeves, both fronts, and the back are all different fabrics. This was fun, and by the time I was finished, I had no leftovers.

5. With right sides together, stitch the underarm seam of the jacket and sleeve. Repeat with the lining. Press seams open.

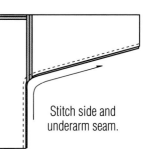

Stitch side and underarm seam.

6. Pin the shoulder pads in place, try on the jacket, and adjust as needed. Sew in place along the shoulder seam by hand and loosely hand tack the corners to the armhole seam allowance.

Tack to jacket foundation.

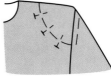
Hand tack to seam allowance.

7. With wrong sides together, pin the lining to the jacket along all raw edges, including the sleeve edges. Open out the binding and turn under ¼" at one end; press. Refold.

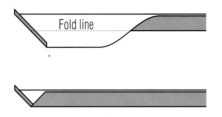

Fold line

8. With right sides together, pin the binding to the neckline, front, and bottom edges, beginning and ending at the center back. Stitch ¼" from the raw edges.

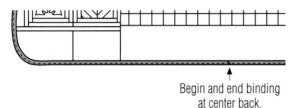

Begin and end binding
at center back.

9. Turn the binding to the inside and slipstitch in place.

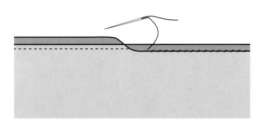

10. Bind the bottom edge of each sleeve in the same manner.
11. Optional: Couch the accent trim next to the finished outer edge of the jacket. (See couching directions on page 49.) Add a frog closure if you wish.

✓A Little Something Extra

Use fabric leftovers to make a bag to match your jacket. Complete directions for making simple bags appear on pages 85–87 of *Jacket Jazz*.

For the smaller purse that matches the longer jacket, I started with a 9" x 18" foundation. I made more Woven Square Strips like the ones used on the left sleeve, then sewed them row by row through the foundation. I inserted the piping near the zipper closing and in one of the seams. I also applied some of the bugle beads and accent trim to the seams.

For the longer purse that matches the shorter jacket, my foundation piece was 11" x 28". First, I created a faced opening in a square of fabric (like the one made for the "Folded Star Block" on page 53), then I placed a piece of one of the whimsical fabrics in my jacket behind the opening. Log Cabin piecing surrounds the square along with a variety of pieces cut from tucked and plain leftovers. Yo-yos and a wooden flower button add the finishing touch.

Mystery Jacket I (Long Version) *by Gloria Seligman, Beaumont, Texas, 1995.*

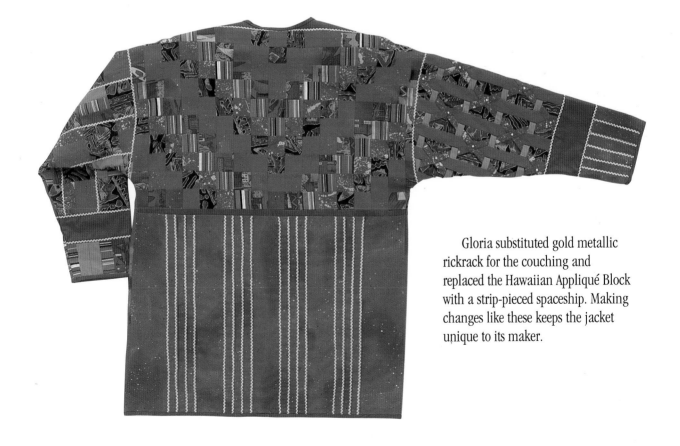

Gloria substituted gold metallic rickrack for the couching and replaced the Hawaiian Appliqué Block with a strip-pieced spaceship. Making changes like these keeps the jacket unique to its maker.

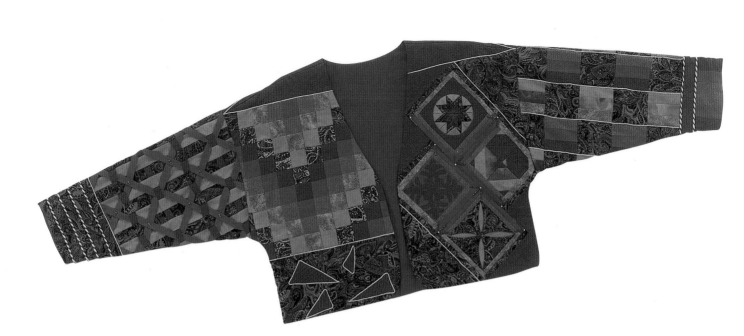

Mystery Jacket I *(Short Version) by Ginny Jones, Houston, Texas, 1994.*

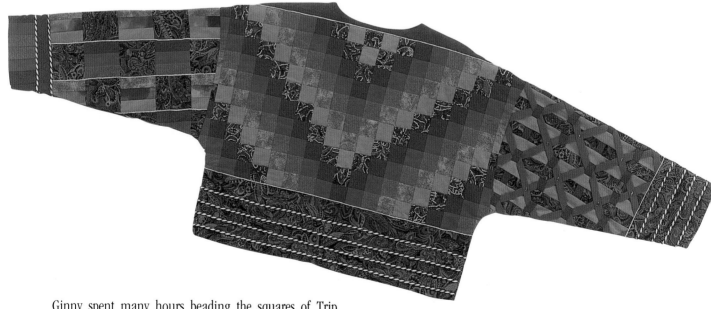

Ginny spent many hours beading the squares of Trip Around the World, following the design in the fabric of one particular square. Ginny worked on this jacket for her mother-in-law during the '94 Olympics, thus its name "Olympic Gold."

√ Templates

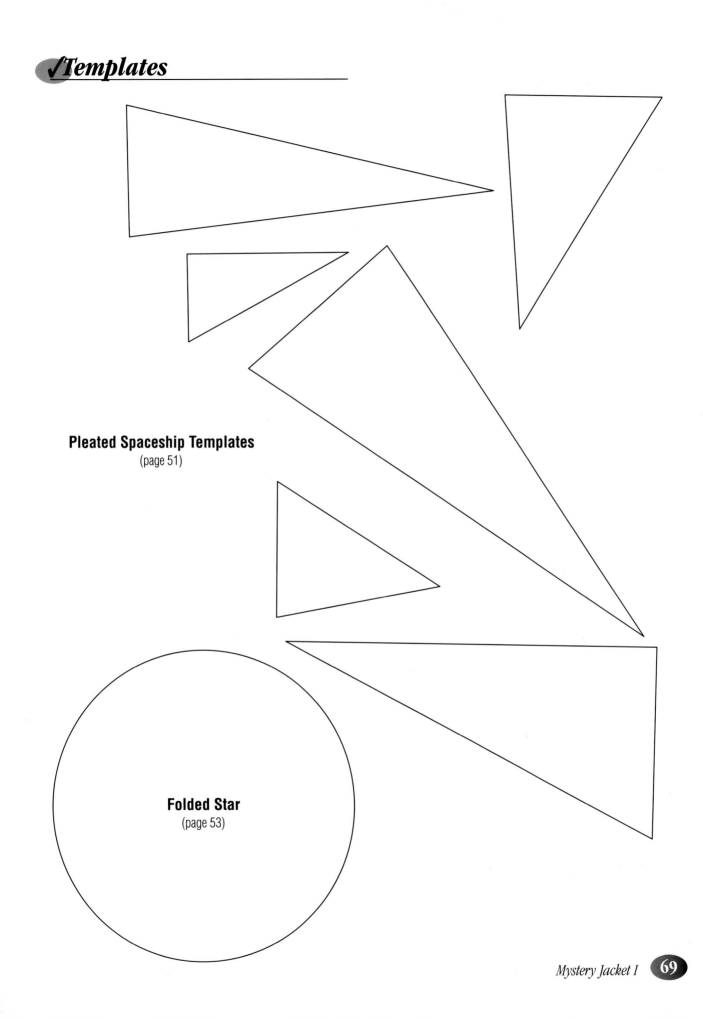

Pleated Spaceship Templates
(page 51)

Folded Star
(page 53)

Linens and Lace

Make this patchwork jacket as frilly as you like or use just a few treasures from Granny's trunk, antique stores, or your collection of special linens and laces.

Linens and Lace Jacket by Judy Murrah.

Shopping List

All yardage requirements are based on 44"-wide fabrics, unless otherwise noted.

Jacket Foundation	3 yds. muslin
Jacket Lining	3 yds. silky lining fabric or smooth cotton fabric
Interfacing	$\frac{1}{2}$ yd. lightweight fusible interfacing
Patchwork Fabrics	$\frac{3}{8}$ yd. each of 8 to 10 fabrics in one or multiple color families (See "Fabric Selection Tips" at right.)
Shoulder Pads	Raglan-style shoulder pads, $\frac{3}{8}$" to $\frac{3}{4}$" thick
Narrow Braid	5 to 8 yds. to cover seams (optional); substitute flat lace if you prefer
Buttons	3 large buttons, $\frac{3}{4}$" to 1" diameter, for front closure
Piping	5 yds. for finishing jacket and sleeve edges
Linens and Laces	Assorted antique doilies, dresser scarves, lace medallions, hankies, lace yardage, lace collars, cuffs, etc.
Embellishments	Trinkets, buttons, and beads as desired
Silk Ribbon or Heirloom Sylk	2 to 3 colors of 4mm-wide ribbon, including green for leaves
Wire-Edged Ribbon	2 yds., $\frac{7}{8}$" wide, in color of your choice for flowers; $\frac{1}{4}$ yd., $\frac{7}{8}$" wide, for leaves
Pearl cotton	Size 8 for feather stitching
Cotton or polyester fiberfill	Small amount for Ribbon Pod

In addition to the fabrics and notions listed, you will need the following special supplies:

    Chenille needles, sizes 18–24, for silk-ribbon embroidery
    Embroidery hoop, 3" to 8" diameter

FABRIC SELECTION TIPS

Anything goes with the fabric selection for this jacket. Select fabrics for the patchwork that are compatible in weight, using silk or lightweight linen suitings, traditional patchwork cottons, dressy rayons and polyesters, or even wool for a more tailored look. When selecting patterned fabrics, choose plaids, stripes, florals, geometric designs, or even solids that work well together.

Note: If you wish to use a fabric that is much lighter in weight than the other fabrics in your selection, back it with a layer of medium-weight fusible interfacing before cutting the necessary pieces from it.

PREPARATION

1. Use the jacket pattern pieces for Jacket Seven in the pullout section in *Jacket Jazz Encore* (or substitute a commercial pattern with similar styling). When tracing the sleeve onto tissue paper, be sure to mark the shoulder notch, the dots on the sleeve cap, and the armhole notches on the jacket front, back, and sleeve for matching purposes.

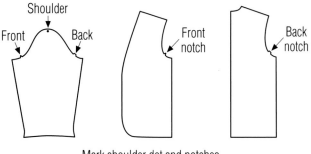

Mark shoulder dot and notches.

2. Cut the jacket back, fronts, and sleeves from the foundation fabric and from the lining. Snip-mark the dots and notches on the front, back, and sleeves. Set the lining pieces aside.

3. Cut lightweight fusible interfacing, using the front and back neckline facing pattern pieces for Jacket Seven. Cut 2"-wide strips for the hem edges of the jacket pieces and the sleeves. Following the manufacturer's directions, apply fusible interfacing to the wrong side of the jacket front and back foundation pieces.

4. Cut and apply the patchwork and add the embellishments, following the directions on pages 79–82.

DIRECTIONS

1. Using your original paper pattern pieces, cut 1 additional sleeve, front, and back pattern piece. Transfer all notches and dots to the pieces. Arrange the pattern pieces on your work surface and mark the left and right front and the left and right sleeve as shown.

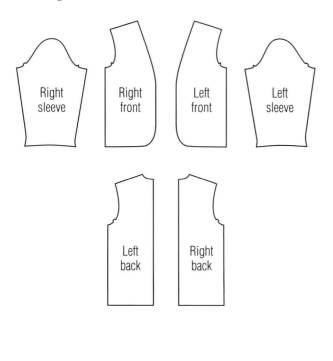

2. Divide both front pattern pieces into 3 sections, drawing the first line (A) perpendicular to the grain line at the underarm. Measure the remaining distance from line A to the bottom edge of the jacket (C) and divide almost in half, making the bottom section 2" longer than the middle section. For example, if the distance from the armhole to the bottom edge is 20", make the second section 8" wide and the third section 12" wide.

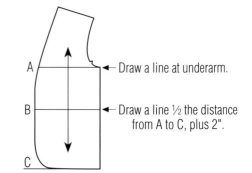

3. Divide the 2 bottom sections in half vertically.

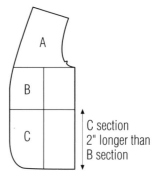

Divide in half vertically.

4. Position the back pattern pieces next to the front at the side seams. Draw a line across each back (D) so it matches line B on the front pattern piece. Then draw a line vertically to divide each back into 4 sections. The finished jacket back will have a total of 8 patchwork pieces, and the fronts will each have 5.

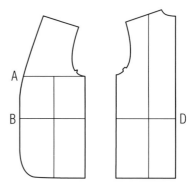

5. Divide the sleeve pattern piece in half by drawing a line at the location of the lengthen/shorten line. (If you are using a commercial pattern, fold the sleeve in half crosswise and crease. Draw a line 1" to 2" below the crease line.) On all pattern pieces, make a ¼" seam notation at each patchwork cutting line (the ones you drew). Write the name of each section on the paper patterns.

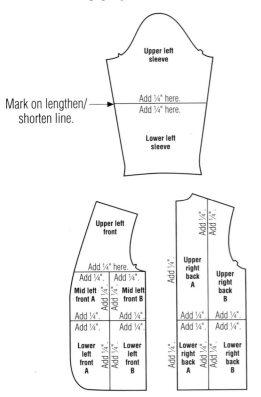

6. Cut each paper pattern into sections and position them, right side up, on the muslin foundation pieces. Pin in place.

7. Decide where you want each of your patchwork fabrics in the completed jacket. Beginning with the left front foundation, cut each patchwork piece from the desired fabric. *To do so, pin the pattern piece right side up to the right side of the fabric. Then place a rotary ruler on top with the ¼" line along the edge of the pattern piece. Cut along the edge of the ruler, thus adding a ¼"-wide seam allowance. Repeat this procedure when cutting any edge that has "Add ¼"" noted.*

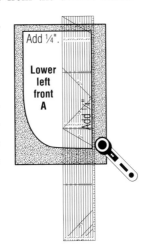

Remove the pattern pieces, one by one, and place the patchwork pieces in their correct position on the left front foundation. Pin in place temporarily. Repeat with the right front.

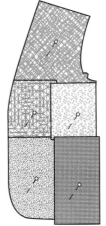

Pin patches to muslin foundation.

8. Gather your linens and laces near the jacket right front and determine which pieces look best with your fabrics. Is white or off-white better with your fabrics? Set aside those pieces that don't work, then choose a linen or lace piece with a pretty corner that you can use as a lapel on the right front. Position it as shown and make sure that it contrasts with the patchwork pieces beneath it. If it doesn't show up well, choose a different piece, or rethink your fabric placements and cut new pieces. Cut linen or lace piece to fit the jacket neckline.

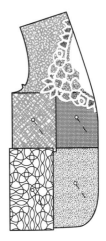

9. Next, cut the pieces for the right sleeve and pin them to the foundation. Choose 2 and position them so that they coordinate well with the patchwork pieces on the right front. If you have lace cuffs or want to simulate them from a piece of linen or lace, pin one in place at the bottom edge of the sleeve after cutting and positioning the patchwork sections on the sleeve. Choose a piece of lace or trim to place where the 2 pieces of patchwork meet. Pin in place. Repeat with the left sleeve.

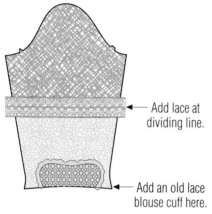

← Add lace at dividing line.

← Add an old lace blouse cuff here.

10. Position the jacket back foundation on your work surface with the fronts and sleeves to each side. Then cut and arrange the 8 patchwork pieces on the foundation. Pay attention to the fabric placement on the back in relation to the fabric on the fronts and sleeves. Pin in place. Choose lace or trim for each of the seam lines and pin near the raw edges.

11. Continue adding linen and lace to the jacket sections to embellish the pieces, pinning them to single or multiple sections of patchwork. Examine the photos on pages 70, 71, and 83 for placement ideas. If the linen or lace piece has raw edges, that's OK; you will catch the edges in the seam lines as you stitch the patchwork pieces in place. If the piece has finished edges, you can simply topstitch these to the garment after stitching the patchwork seams.

Stand back and evaluate your composition, making sure that both sides are balanced—for example, not too much froufrou on one side in comparison to the other. Look for color balance too. Since nothing is stitched in place yet, it's not too late to change your mind about a piece or two of the patchwork.

When you are pleased with your arrangement, you are ready to complete each garment section. Choose one of the following methods or a combination of them as it suits your arrangement of fabrics, linens, and lace to stitch the pieces to the foundation.

METHOD I

Use this method when a piece of linen or lace must be inserted in the seam of the patchwork because it has raw edges.

1. Pin the patchwork fabric (A) in place, right side up, on the foundation. Pin the linen or lace to the raw edge of the fabric with edges even.

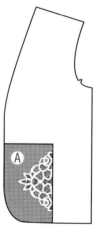

Pin lace even with raw edge of fabric.

2. Pin the next fabric (B) in place with right sides together and raw edges even. Stitch ¼" from the raw edges. Flip the fabric onto the foundation and press. Position the lace on top of the patchwork A and pin in place.

Note: If you are adding a piece of linen or lace to a section of patchwork that's made up of two fabric pieces, stitch the fabric pieces together first, press the seam open or to one side, and add the piece to the foundation, followed by the lace.

Stitch together.

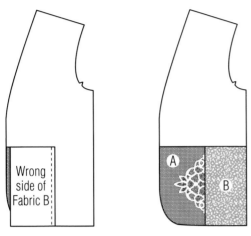

Wrong side of Fabric B

Flip B to right side.

3. Stitch ⅛" from the raw edges of the foundation to anchor the fabric. Hand appliqué or machine stitch the loose edges of the lace in place as desired.

METHOD II

Use this method when a piece of linen or lace with finished edges will be machine or hand appliquéd in place *on top* of the patchwork pieces.

1. Position the first fabric on the foundation and pin in place.
2. Place the next patchwork piece face down on the right side of the first with raw edges even and stitch ¼" from the raw edges as shown in step 2 for Method 1.
3. Flip the second piece onto the foundation; press, pin, and stitch ⅛" from the raw edges. Position the linen or lace on the completed patchwork where desired and edgestitch in place. It may be necessary to hand stitch more delicate pieces in place so the stitching doesn't show and to avoid damaging them.

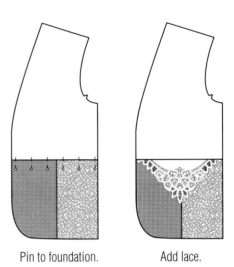

Pin to foundation.   Add lace.

EMBELLISHING YOUR JACKET

Now it's time to gussy up your creation, adding trinkets, buttons, beads and trim, more lace if desired, and stitchery, including silk-ribbon embroidery. Examine the photos of the jackets on pages 70, 71, and 83 for ideas.

1. After all pieces are attached to the foundation, stitch the desired trim(s) in place on top of the patchwork seam lines.
2. Add desired embellishments, sewing them on by hand. Directions for several ribbon embellishments and embroidery stitches begin on page 79. You can add these now or after the jacket is completed.

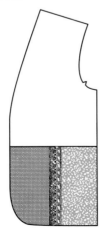

Add lace to finished seam.

✓ Jacket Finishing

Use ½"-wide seam allowances.

1. With right sides together, stitch the jacket fronts to the back at the shoulders. Repeat with the jacket lining pieces. Cover the seam line of the patchwork jacket with trim if desired.

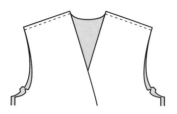

2. Arrange the jacket on top of the wrong side of the lining. If the lining is larger than the jacket, trim it even with the jacket edges.

3. Machine baste from notch to notch along the seam line on each jacket and lining sleeve cap. Pin the sleeves to the jacket armholes, matching notches and the center dot to the shoulder seam line. Draw up the basting stitches to fit. Adjust gathers evenly. Stitch. Remove the basting. Repeat with the lining sleeves.

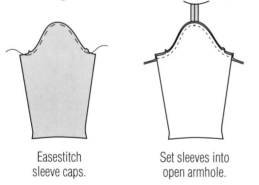

Easestitch sleeve caps.　　Set sleeves into open armhole.

4. Press the seams toward the sleeves in the jacket and lining. On the right side, cover the jacket sleeve seam with trim if desired. With the jacket right sides together, stitch the side seams, continuing to the bottom edge of the sleeve. Press the seams open. Repeat with the lining.

5. Carefully steam press the completed jacket, being careful not to flatten the lace or embroidery.

6. Pin the shoulder pads inside the jacket, try on, and adjust as necessary. Sew the shoulder pads to the shoulder seam by hand and loosely hand-tack the corners to the armhole seam allowance.

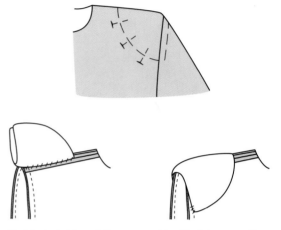

Tack to jacket foundation.　　Hand tack to seam allowance.

7. Beginning at the center back, pin and baste the piping to the outer edges of the jacket, positioning the piping cord ½" from the cut edge of the jacket. Overlap the ends as shown when you reach the starting point. Repeat at the bottom edge of each sleeve, starting and ending the piping close to the underarm seam. Press the seam allowance toward the foundation side of the sleeve. (No patchwork is shown in the jacket illustration below.)

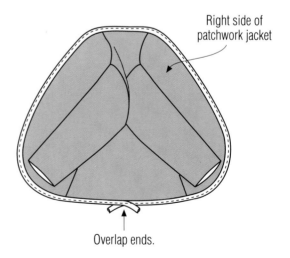

Right side of patchwork jacket

Overlap ends.

8. Pin the lining to the outer edges of the jacket front and back, with right sides together and raw edges matching. Stitch, using a zipper foot or cording to get close to the cording. Begin and end the stitching on the back 3" from each side seam, leaving an opening for turning.

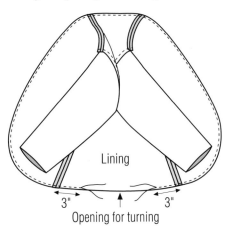

9. Trim the seam allowance to ¼", clip the neckline curves, and turn the jacket right side out through the opening at the bottom edge. Press carefully. Turn in the lining at the lower edge of the jacket back and slipstitch to the piping.

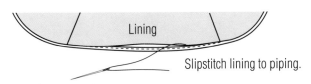

10. Turn under and press ½" at the bottom edge of each sleeve lining. Slipstitch to the piping.

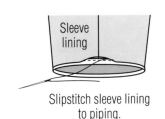

11. Make buttonholes in the positions indicated on the pattern and sew buttons in place on the left front.

✓Silk-Ribbon Embroidery

You can use silk ribbon or Heirloom Sylk by Mokuba to work most standard embroidery stitches. The following stitching tips will help. You might want to practice first on some scraps.

- To give the finished stitches a soft, three-dimensional look, it's important not to pull the ribbon tight; instead, allow the stitches to rest gently on the fabric. After piercing the fabric with the needle, eliminate any kinks by smoothing the underside of the ribbon with a large, blunt needle, such as a tapestry needle.

- To reduce raveling and fraying, work with pieces of ribbon about 12" long. After threading the needle with ribbon, push the needle point through this same end of ribbon about ¼" from one end. Pull on the long end to lock the ribbon in place on the needle.

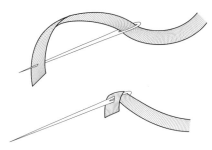

- To make a knot in the other end of the ribbon, form a circle with the end of the ribbon and the point of the needle. Fold the end back on itself, pierce both layers with the needle close to the fold, then pull the needle and the ribbon through both layers to form a soft knot.

- To end an area of stitching, work a couple of small backstitches into the ribbon or fabric on the wrong side.
- If you like, you can draw the design on your fabric before you start stitching. I just stitch as I please with a plan in mind. That way, there aren't any lines that I must be sure to hide as I stitch.

Spider Web Rose

1. Using a single strand of matching embroidery floss or regular sewing thread, make 5 spokes of equal length as shown in the diagram. Start with a fly stitch to make the first 3 spokes. Then add the 2 remaining spokes.

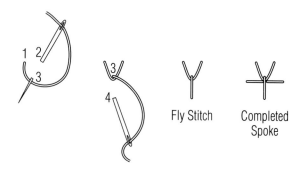

Fly Stitch   Completed Spoke

2. Thread the needle with ribbon and make a soft knot at the end. Bring the needle through the fabric from the wrong side, coming up at the center of the spoke. Twist the needle about 5 times to twist the ribbon; weave over and under the spokes, allowing the ribbon to form a gentle fold in each section. Repeat around the spokes until they are covered. Add French knots (at right) to the center if you wish.

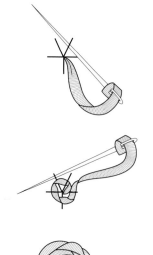

French Knots

1. Thread the needle with ribbon of the desired color. Bring the needle up through the fabric from the wrong side.
2. Wrap the ribbon once or twice around the needle. Hold the ribbon off to one side as you insert the needle in the fabric as close to the starting point as possible. Hold the knot in place until the needle is pulled through. For a loftier bud, wrap the needle 3 to 6 times. Insert the needle back into the fabric as close to the starting point as possible. Don't pull the ribbon tight; let the knot remain loose and flowery.

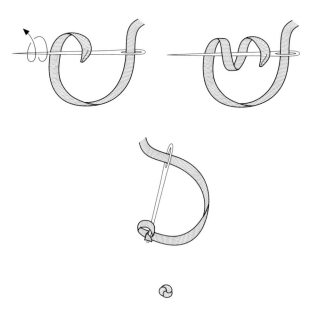

Japanese Ribbon Stitch

Use this stitch to make leaves of varying length to go with your flowers.
1. With ribbon in the needle, bring it up from under the fabric at point A. Lay the ribbon flat on the fabric and pierce the ribbon in the center at point B.

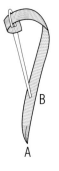

2. Gently (not too tight) pull the needle through to the back. The ribbon will curl at the tip. Stop pulling before you pull the curl out.

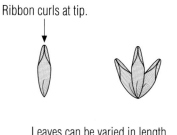

Ribbon curls at tip.

Leaves can be varied in length to go with your flower.

Detached Chain (Lazy Daisy)

You may vary the length of the loop and the stitch that anchors the loop. Use for petals and leaves.
1. With ribbon in the needle, bring it from the back of the fabric to the front and hold the ribbon flat with your thumb. Insert the needle at the starting point and on top of the ribbon so a loop forms.
2. Bring the needle back through the fabric a short distance from the top of the loop. Pass the needle over the ribbon and back into the fabric. This stitch anchors the top of the loop.

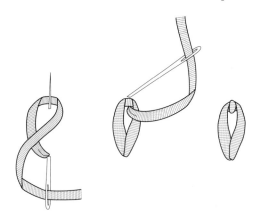

Feather Stitch (for pearl cotton)

This is a vertical stitch that alternates from right to left and is worked from top to bottom with pearl cotton. Refer to the illustration following step 2 above right.
1. Begin with a single stitch. Come up at A and down at B, but don't pull the thread tight yet. Come up in the center below A and B, at C. The secret is to always put the needle in at B straight across from where the thread came out at A.

2. To make a trail of flowering vines, do a single stitch or several stitches to the right and then to the left. Build your flowers next to and around the vine. Add buds (French knots) to the open end of each feather stitch.

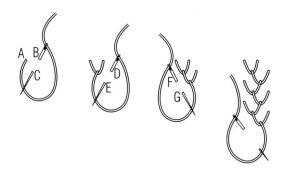

Antique Ribbon Rose

1. Cut a 24"-long piece of $\frac{7}{8}$"-wide, wire-edged ribbon. Fold ribbon in half crosswise and hold the raw edges with one hand. With the other hand, pull the 2 wires on the bottom edge to gather the ribbon to about $\frac{1}{3}$ its original length. Unfold the ribbon.

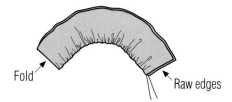

Fold   Raw edges

2. Pinch the end of the ribbon and wrap with the long wire $\frac{1}{4}$" from the raw edge. Trim excess wire if necessary. Repeat at the other end.

Linens and Lace

3. Fold one end down below the bottom edge of the ribbon and use like a handle. Wrap the ribbon around itself tightly 3 times at the end. Using matching thread, whipstitch the bottom edges together. Continue to roll the next layer; hand sew it just to the previous ribbon layer. Gradually move the gathered wire ⅛" out from the roll before. Keep tacking the rows as you go.

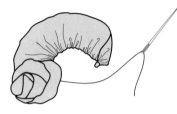

4. When you come to the end of the ribbon, pull it to the back and stitch it in place.
5. Place the rose in the palm of your hand and and squeeze it with your fingertips as if you were trying to squeeze water out of it. Gently straighten it out and primp the edges, leaving the crinkle in the rose.
6. Pin the finished rose in place on the garment with a leaf behind it (see below). Hand stitch the rose and leaf in place from the back side with matching thread and small, hidden stitches.

RIBBON LEAF

Cut a 2"-long piece of ⅞"-wide, wire-edged ribbon. Fold the raw edges on both sides to one finished edge. Pinch in the center and stitch to hold. Place under an antique ribbon rose and stitch in place.

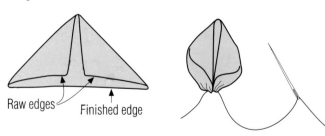

Raw edges   Finished edge

RIBBON POD

Note: You may use wire-edged ribbon for this if you remove the wire.

1. Use a 4½"-long piece of ⅞"-wide ribbon. Fold the ribbon in half and stitch the cut ends together. Turn the ribbon right side out and finger-press.
2. Do a gathering stitch right below the top selvage edge. Pull the gathers tight and tack it closed.
3. Do a gathering stitch along the bottom edge. Do not pull up yet. Firmly stuff the pod with cotton or polyester fiberfill.

Sew ends together.

Fiberfill stuffing

4. Pull the bottom thread to gather and close the pod. Backstitch. Tack firmly to your garment.

Backstitch to secure stitches.

Note: I made two antique roses with leaves and a pod next to them on the upper left front of one of my jackets, then added a trail of feather stitching with Spider Web Roses and French knot buds.

Linens and Lace
by Tenna Thompson,
Victoria, Texas, 1995.

Tenna used an inherited, family collection of vintage lace and a monochromatic color scheme to create this keepsake jacket.

Silk-ribbon embroidery flowers embellish the lower part of the sleeves as well as the right front collar area.

Spring Has Sprung

◆ *Slice of Heaven*

◆ *My Lady's Fan*

◆ *The Garden Path*

◆ *Stepping-stones*

Directions for three vests are included in this section. "Spring Has Sprung" and "Christmas Celebration" are obviously seasonal. However, if you choose country plaids in autumn colors and replace the Christmas embellishments with other appliquéd designs, you'll have a wonderful vest for fall. Look for small ceramic buttons and charms in harvest themes—pumpkins, scarecrows—to embellish the vest. Christmas fabrics and a bit of lamé could turn the spring vest into another Christmas version, or choose pretty florals for a summer vest.

"Seven Easy Pieces" can be made to look like any season, depending on your fabric choices. The version shown on page 104 would make a great summer vest in its patriotic colors. Choose your favorite colors and fabrics and make a vest for each season or special holiday, embellishing the patchwork to your heart's content.

✓*Spring Has Sprung Construction at a Glance*

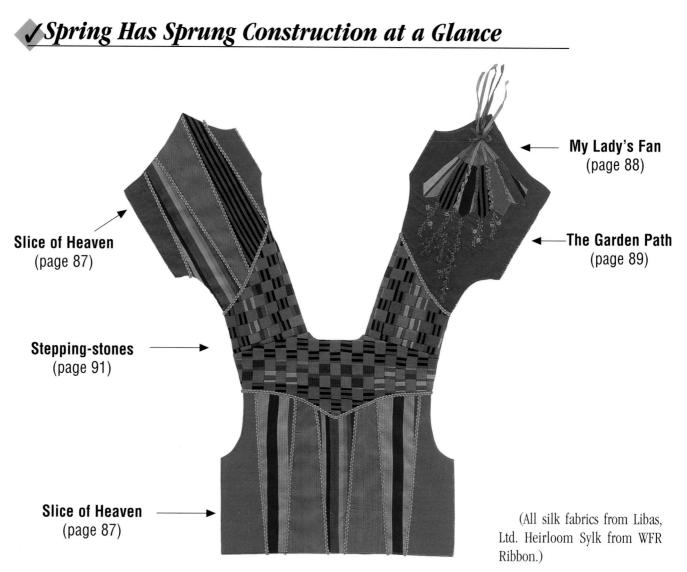

Slice of Heaven
(page 87)

Stepping-stones
(page 91)

Slice of Heaven
(page 87)

My Lady's Fan
(page 88)

The Garden Path
(page 89)

(All silk fabrics from Libas, Ltd. Heirloom Sylk from WFR Ribbon.)

Spring Has Sprung Vest by Judy Murrah.

PREPARATION

Use a commercial vest pattern with styling similar to those shown in the photos or use the body of Jacket Six from *Jacket Jazz Encore*. Set aside any facing pattern pieces as you will not need them, unless you wish to use them to cut the interfacing.

1. Cut the vest pieces from muslin for the foundation and from the lining. Cut 2½"-wide strips of fusible interfacing and fuse to the wrong side of the foundation front. To make straight strips fit, make wedge-shaped cutouts at the inner edge of the interfacing.

2. Draw a yoke on the muslin fronts and back. You may adapt the yoke pattern from Jacket Ten in *Jacket Jazz Encore* as a guide, or refer to the illustration below.

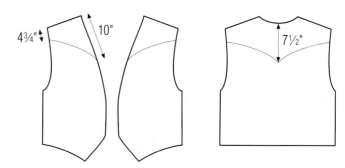

4¾"   10"   7½"

Draw yoke lines on muslin fronts and back.

Shopping List

All yardage requirements are based on 44"-wide fabrics, unless otherwise noted.

Vest Foundation	1¼ yds. muslin
Vest Lining, Fabric #7	1¼ yds. smooth cotton fabric
Interfacing	¼ yd. lightweight fusible interfacing
Patchwork Fabrics #1–#6	¼ yd. each of 6 different contrasting fabrics, including 1 each of a small, medium, and large print
Appliqué Fabric #8	½ yd. or a piece large enough to cover right vest front
Piping	3 to 4 yds. to finish outer edges
Silk Ribbon or Heirloom Sylk	3 to 5 colors, 4mm wide, that coordinate with pieced fan to embroider flowers
Satin Ribbon	2 yds. each of 5 different ribbons, ranging in size from ⅛" to ⅞" wide
Trim or Braid	2 yds. to outline yoke
Beads	As desired to embellish fan
Assorted Buttons	As desired to embellish left front
Pearl Cotton (size 8) or Embroidery Floss	For feather-stitched vine on vest front
Elastic	½" wide and 6" to 8" long for back

In addition to the fabrics and notions listed, you will need the following special supplies:

- 9° Circle Wedge Ruler
- Chenille needles, sizes 18–24, for silk-ribbon embroidery
- Embroidery hoop, 3" to 8" diameter
- Template plastic for pieced fan

Slice of Heaven

(Back and Left Front)

MATERIALS

⅛ yd. each of 5 different fabrics
1 yd. each of 5 different satin ribbons or Heirloom Sylk
Assorted buttons for embellishment

DIRECTIONS

1. Determine the order in which you want to use the 5 fabrics to make the wedges. Arrange them so right and left halves of the back are mirror images, or arrange them randomly as you wish. You will cut each wedge as you are ready to stitch it to the vest foundation.

2. Center the wide end of the 9° wedge ruler at the point of the yoke line, with the top edge of the ruler 1" above the yoke line on each side as shown. Note the length.

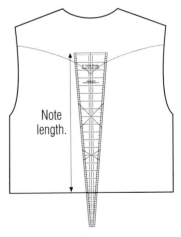

Measure from yoke line with 9° wedge ruler.

3. Use the 9° wedge ruler to cut a wedge from the desired fabric equal to this length, starting at the wide end of the ruler. (You will cut all additional wedges, starting at the wide end of the ruler.) Pin the wedge to the foundation, right side up, centering it and making sure that it covers the yoke line at each outer edge. Trim the upper edge of the wedge even with the yoke line, and the bottom end even with the bottom edge of the vest back.

4. Place the wide end of the ruler at the bottom edge of the vest and measure for the length of Wedges #2 and #3 in the same manner, adding 1" extra to the measurement. Cut Wedges #2 and #3.

5. With the wide ends of Wedges #2 and #3 at the bottom edge of the vest back, arrange them to check the positioning. Make sure that the wedges extend above the yoke line. Pin Wedge #3 in place temporarily. Carefully flip Wedge #2 over on top of Wedge #1 and pin in place with raw edges even. Stitch through all layers ¼" from the raw edges. End the stitching at the yoke line. Flip the wedge onto the foundation; press and pin in place. Trim the upper edge even with the yoke line. Repeat with Wedge #3.

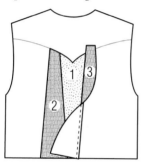

6. Continue cutting, adding, and trimming wedges to cover the back and left front from the yoke lines to the bottom edge of the foundation. Cover each seam line with ribbon, using a straight or decorative embroidery stitch. If you wish, hand couch the ribbons in place as shown on page 29. Add a row of buttons to the second and third wedges of the vest front if you wish.

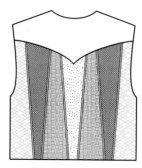

Cover seams with ribbon trim.

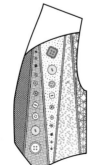

Add button embellishment to Wedges #2 and #3.

✓My Lady's Fan

(Right Front)

MATERIALS

A piece of Fabric #7 large enough to cover right front foundation from yoke line to bottom edge
Scraps of Fabrics #1–#7 for fan
Template plastic

DIRECTIONS

Use Templates A and B on page 94.

1. Cut a piece of Fabric #7 to cover the right front from the yoke line to the bottom edge. Place the piece, right side up, on top of the foundation; stitch ⅛" from the outer raw edges.

2. Trace Templates A and B onto template plastic.

3. Using Template B, cut a total of 6 different fan blades. Using Template A, cut 1 fan center from Fabric #7.

4. Fold each fan segment right sides together with long edges even. Stitch ¼" from the edge of the wider end of each blade. Clip the corners, press the seams open, and turn right side out. Press.

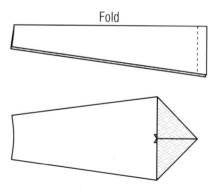

Fold

5. Sew the 6 blades together along the long edges, using a ¼"-wide seam allowance. Press seams to one side.

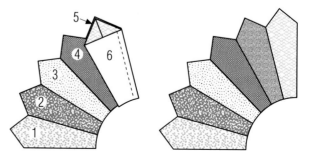

6. With right sides together and raw edges even, pin the fan center to the fan, matching the dot on the fan center to the center seam of the fan. Pin the outer edges of the fan center even with the outer edges of the fan. With the fan on the bottom, stitch ¼" from the raw edges, stretching the fan center as necessary to fit the curved edge of the fan. Press the seam toward the center. Turn under and press ¼" on the fan outer edges.

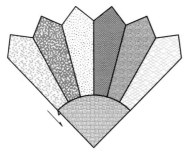

7. Referring to the photos on pages 84 and 86, position the fan on the right front, with the bottom point in line with the vest point. Machine stitch the straight edges of the fan in place, using a decorative stitch. The top of the fan will remain unstitched until the ribbon embellishments have been added. See "The Garden Path" above right.

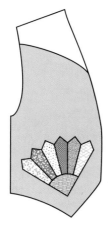

Points in line

✓*The Garden Path*

(Right Front)

MATERIALS

3 to 5 different colors of 4mm-wide silk ribbon or Heirloom Sylk

5 colors of satin ribbon or Heirloom Sylk, ⅛" to ⅞" wide, for fan embellishment

Beads for fan embellishment

Chenille needles in any size from 18–24

3"- to 8"-diameter embroidery hoop

Embroidery floss or size 8 pearl cotton for embroidered vines

DIRECTIONS

To embellish the fan blades, add ribbon to each seam line as shown below, *ending the stitching at the lower edge of each fan blade and leaving a long tail of ribbon for streamers.* See step 5 on next page to complete the ribbon streamers.

1. Cover each of the fan seams with satin ribbon, placing the raw end under the edge of the fan before stitching. Cover 1 seam using the technique for "Crisscross Hand-Couched Ribbon" on page 29. Cover another with "Gathered Rosettes" as shown on page 30.

2. For the third seam, ruche the ribbon before stitching it to the fan. With matching thread, hand stitch in zigzag fashion as shown, leaving the needle and thread attached when you reach the end. Draw up the thread, gathering the ribbon to fit the fan seam line and leaving a long tail at the end for the streamer. Secure the gathers with a few backstitches. Pin along the fan seam line and hand tack in place.

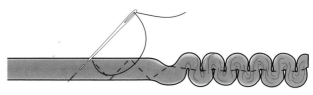

Stitch in a V line.

◀ **Note:** For a different effect, stack two ribbons of different colors and widths before you do the stitching. Vary the degree of waviness in the ribbon by varying the stitch length and angularity of the zigzag stitching.

3. For another seam, make pinched couching. Thread a needle with a double strand of thread. Beginning at the top edge of the fan, place the raw end of the ribbon under the edge of the fan, with the ribbon along the seam line. Bring the needle through from the back, slightly under one edge of the ribbon and ¼" from the top edge of the fan. Move the needle across the ribbon and down through the vest, slightly under the ribbon edge. Take several small stitches over the ribbon, pulling each stitch tight so the ribbon draws in.

   For the next stitch, bring the needle through the vest from the wrong side, ½" from the first couching stitches. Stitch across the ribbon as before. Continue in this manner, couching at ½" intervals until you reach the bottom of the fan blades. If you wish, add beads as you stitch.

Take several stitches in place.

Pinched Couching

4. Do the French Knot Twist along the length of the last seam: Thread a needle with a double strand of pearl cotton, embroidery floss, or a single strand of silk ribbon; knot the end. Tuck the end of the ribbon under the top edge of the fan. Bring the needle up from the wrong side of the foundation into the ribbon. Make a French knot as shown on page 80. Twist the ribbon, allowing a little slack, and tack down with another French knot. Continue twisting and tacking at irregular intervals. If you prefer, substitute small beads for the French knots.

Twist and tack ribbon with French knots.

5. Draw the ribbon tails together at the fan point and tack in place with a bow made from a length of ⅛"- or ¼"-wide ribbon. Allow ribbons to hang 4" to 5" below the bottom edge of the vest front. Tie a "love knot" at the end of each ribbon and trim the end at an angle.

6. Machine stitch the top edge of the fan in place as you did the side edges, using a decorative machine-embroidery stitch.

7. Embellish the curved edge of the fan center with 6 to 8 gathered ribbon roses. For each rose, cut a 4" length of ¼"-wide ribbon. Fold the ribbon in half crosswise with right sides together. Stitch the short ends together in a narrow seam. Do a short running stitch close to one finished edge of the ribbon, leaving the needle and thread attached. Draw up the stitches to gather the ribbon. Backstitch to secure.

Gather one edge to make a rose.

   To make a leaf twist for each ribbon flower, cut a 1¼" length of ⅛"-wide ribbon. Fold to form half of a figure eight. Tack ends together. Tuck a leaf behind each rose as you tack it in place on the vest, adding a tiny bead or two in the stitching if you wish.

Leaf Twist

8. Referring to the photo on page 84, feather stitch 2 paths above the fan. (See page 81 for feather-stitching directions.) Embellish with roses, leaves, and French knots done in silk-ribbon embroidery as shown on pages 79–81.

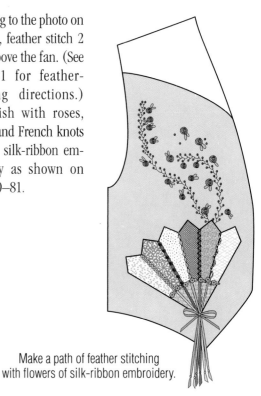

Make a path of feather stitching with flowers of silk-ribbon embroidery.

✓Stepping-stones

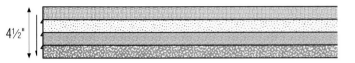

(Front and Back Yokes)

MATERIALS

3 strips, each 1½" x 42", of 4 different fabrics (12 strips total)

DIRECTIONS

1. Sew 4 strips together. to make a strip-pieced unit that measures 4½" x 42". Press the seams in one direction. Repeat with the remaining strips to make a total of 3 identical strip-pieced units.

4½"

Make 3 strip-pieced units.

2. Cut 3 segments, each 14" long, from each strip-pieced unit. If your strip units are less than 42" long, cut the units into 3 pieces of equal length. Sew the segments together to make 3 identical strip-pieced units.

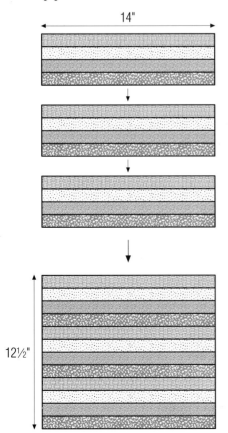

14"

12½"

Make 3 identical strip-pieced units.

3. Working with one unit at a time, cut each strip unit into 1½"-wide segments. You should get 8 to 10 segments from each unit. Leave the segments in the order cut. After you have cut the entire unit into segments, reverse every other strip so unlike blocks are touching each other.

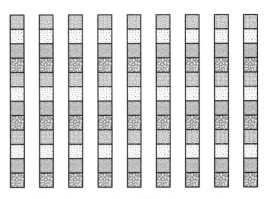

Cut each strip unit into 1½"-wide segments.

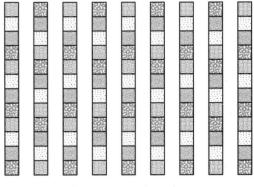

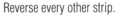

Reverse every other strip.

4. Sew the strips back together again. You should have 3 identical pieced units.

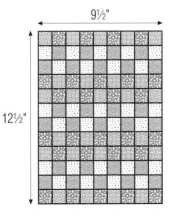

9½"

12½"

Resew strips together to make
3 identical pieces of patchwork.

Spring Has Sprung 91

5. Sew the units together to make one long piece of patchwork, approximately 12½" x 27½".

6. If you did not use the yoke pattern from *Jacket Jazz Encore*, trace the yoke shape you drew on your back and front vest pieces onto tracing paper and cut out. You should have 1 back and 2 fronts. If you used the pattern from *Jacket Jazz Encore*, trace the front yoke pattern onto tracing paper and cut it out so you have a right and left front yoke. Pin the back yoke pattern to the patchwork. Pin the front yoke pattern pieces to the patchwork. Cut out all 3 pieces.

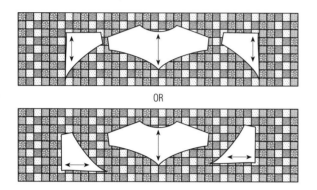

7. Position the yokes on the foundation, pin in place, and stitch ⅛" from all raw edges. Cover the raw edges where they meet at the yoke with trim.

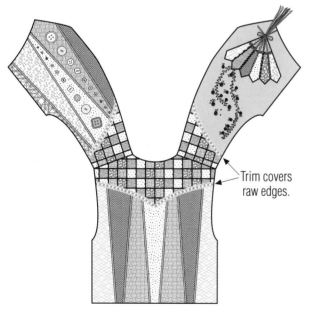

Trim covers raw edges.

✓ Vest Finishing

Use ½"-wide seams.

1. Staystitch a scant ½" from the raw edge of the vest back neckline. Clip curves to, but not through, the staystitching.

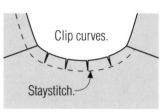

Clip curves.

Staystitch.

2. With right sides together, sew the vest fronts to the vest back at the shoulders. Repeat with the lining. Press seams open.

3. Pin and baste piping to the outer edges of the vest, positioning the piping cord ½" from the cut edge of the vest. Position one piece across the lower vest back. Position another piece, beginning and ending at the lower front side edges. Repeat at the armhole edges, angling the piping into the seam allowance at the underarm.

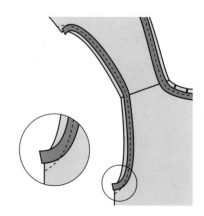

Angle piping off vest armhole and side seam at ½" stitching line.

4. With right sides together, pin the lining to the vest with shoulder seams matching and all outer edges even. Stitch the lining to the vest, leaving the side seams open for turning. Clip curves and corners.

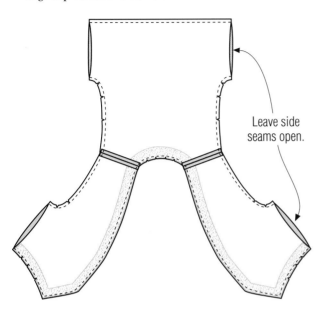

Leave side seams open.

5. Turn the vest right side out by pulling the fronts through the shoulders and out one of the back side openings as shown. Press carefully.

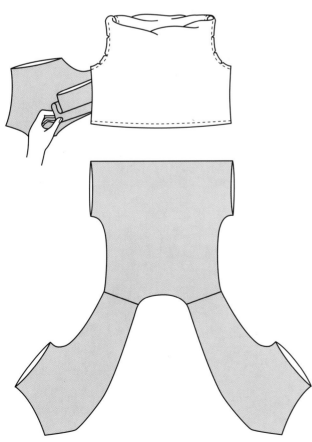

6 With right sides together and raw edges even, pin the vest front to the back at the sides, matching the armhole and lower-edge seam lines. Starting on the lining 1" above the armhole seam, stitch the side seams, ending on the lining 1" below the seam at the bottom edge of the vest as shown.

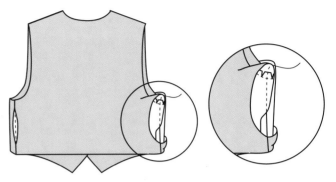

7. Try on the vest and mark your waistline with a horizontal pin at the center back. (It's easier if you have someone to help.) Remove the vest and, on the lining side, draw a $4\frac{1}{2}$"-long line from the pin to each side of the center back. Draw a second line $\frac{3}{4}$" above it. Stitch on each line, backstitching at the beginning and end.

9"

Stitch on lines through vest and lining.

8. Attach a safety pin to one end of the elastic. Reaching through one side-seam opening, insert the safety pin into the casing and work it through to the opposite end, being careful to secure each end of the elastic with a pin at the end of the casing. Stitch in place several times; remove all pins.

9. Press the side seams toward the back. Turn under the side seam allowances on the lining back and blindstitch to the lining along the front side-seam allowance.

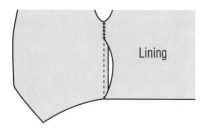

10. Press the vest one final time, then put that smart-looking thing on your back and take off like you're the hottest thing going! And by all means, have fun shopping for the fabric for your Christmas vest. You'll probably want to make more than one for gifts, so it's never too early to start your Christmas sewing.

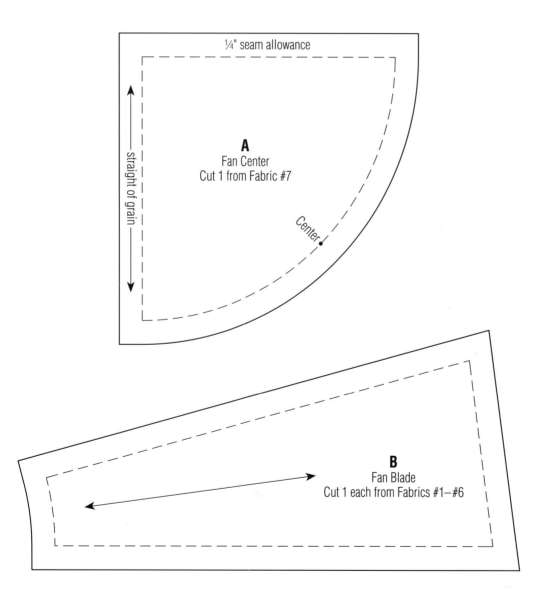

¼" seam allowance

straight of grain

A
Fan Center
Cut 1 from Fabric #7

Center

B
Fan Blade
Cut 1 each from Fabrics #1–#6

Spring Has Sprung
by Inez Libersat, Nederland, Texas, 1995.

Inez repeated the fan shape on the back of her vest by placing the short ends of the wedges together instead of alternating them as I did in the original design.

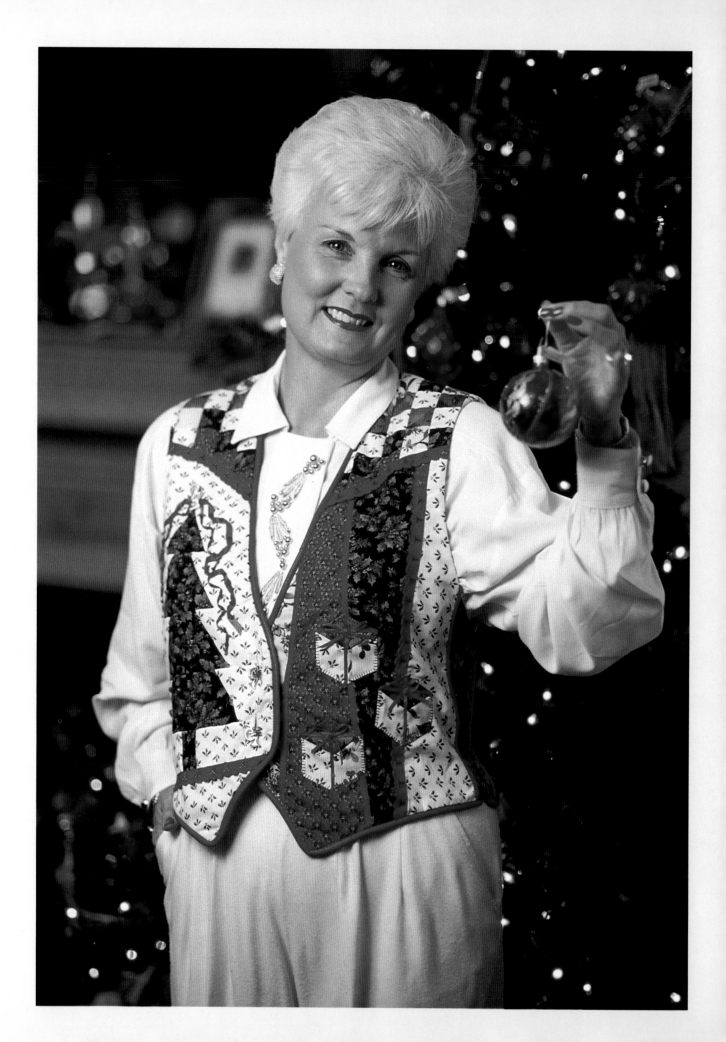

Christmas Celebration

◆ **Slice of Heaven**

◆ **Bow-Tied Packages**

◆ **Oh, Christmas Tree**

◆ **Christmas Presents**

✔Christmas Celebration Construction at a Glance

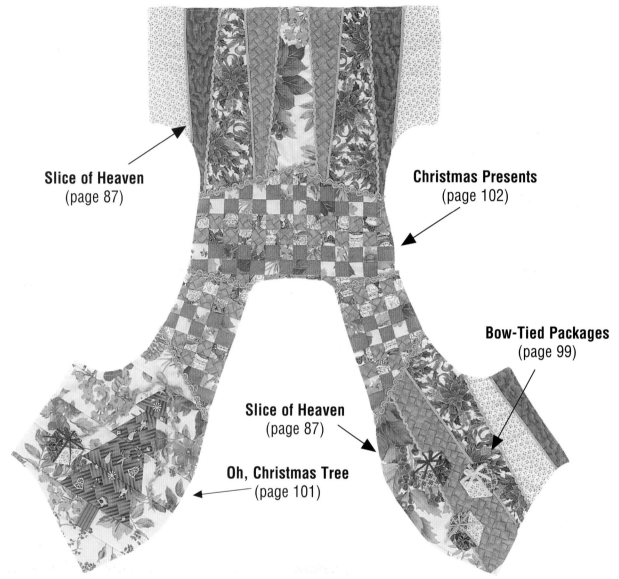

Slice of Heaven
(page 87)

Christmas Presents
(page 102)

Bow-Tied Packages
(page 99)

Slice of Heaven
(page 87)

Oh, Christmas Tree
(page 101)

Christmas Celebration Vest by Barbara Weiland.

PREPARATION

Refer to the preparation directions for "Spring Has Sprung" on page 86.

✔Slice of Heaven

(Left Front and Back)

MATERIALS

⅛ yd. each of 5 different fabrics
1 yd. each of 5 different ribbons

DIRECTIONS

Follow the directions for "Slice of Heaven" on page 87, omitting the button embellishments on the left vest front.

Shopping List

All yardage requirements are based on 44"-wide fabrics, unless otherwise noted.

Vest Foundation	1¼ yds. muslin
Vest Lining Fabric	1¼ yds. smooth cotton fabric
Interfacing	¼ yd. lightweight fusible interfacing
Piecing Fabrics	¼ yd. each of 5 different, contrasting fabrics, including a light, medium, and dark fabric; a small, medium, and large print; and a green for Christmas tree
Background for Tree	¼ yd. light-colored fabric
Lightweight Woven Interfacing	⅛ yd.
Piping	3 to 4 yds. to finish outer edges
Ribbon Trim	2 yds. each of 5 ribbons in assorted colors or textures, ranging in size from ⅛" to ½" wide
Trim or Braid	2 yds. to outline yoke
Beads and Tiny Bells	As desired to adorn tree and packages
Button or Charm	For tree topper
Buttons (optional)	2 buttons, ½" to ⅝" diameter, for front closure
Elastic	½" wide and 6" to 8" long

In addition to the fabrics and notions listed, you will need the following special supplies:

> 9° Circle Wedge Ruler
> 60° triangle ruler, such as the Clear View Triangle™ by Sara Nephew
> Template plastic or cardboard

Bow-Tied Packages

(Left Front)

MATERIALS

1¾" x 14" strip each of a light, medium, and dark fabric
1 yd. of ⅛"-wide ribbon or trim to tie bows
⅛ yd. lightweight fusible interfacing
4 tiny bells
Template plastic

DIRECTIONS

Use the template on page 102.

1. Trace the diamond template on page 102 onto template plastic and cut it out.
2. Stack the 1¾"-wide strips on top of each other with right sides facing up and raw edges even. Place the diamond template on top of the strips and cut through all layers, using a rotary cutter and ruler. Repeat 3 times. You will have 4 light-, 4 medium-, and 4 dark-colored diamonds.

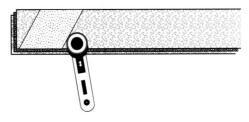

3. On the wrong side of each diamond, mark the seam intersections with cross hairs, using a sharp pencil.

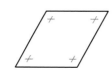

Mark seam intersections on wrong side.

4. Arrange the pieces for a total of 4 packages.

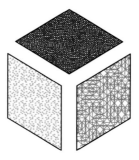

Arrange pieces for 4 "packages."

5. With right sides together, sew a dark and medium diamond together for each package, ending at the marked seam intersection.

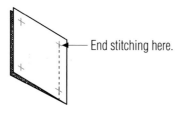

— End stitching here.

6. Add the light diamond, stitching from the seam intersection to the outer edge.

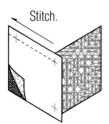

Stitch.

7. Sew the remaining seam, stitching from the center out. Press all seams toward the dark diamond, which is the package top. Trim away the seam points that extend beyond the outer edges.

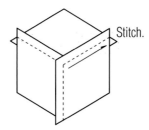

Stitch.

8. Center ribbon or trim over the seam, continuing up to the point. Stitch a second piece across the first, positioning as shown on the template so the ribbon extends from point to point after finishing the boxes as directed below.

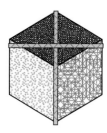

Stitch ribbon to package.

9. Using the finished boxes as patterns, place each one right side up on the fusible side of the interfacing. Pin in place and cut out.

10. With each box right side down on the nonfusible side of its interfacing piece, stitch ¼" from the raw edges around the entire piece. Trim the corners. Make a slit in the interfacing and pull the box right side out through the slit. Make sure points are pushed out smoothly. Press from the right side of the box, making sure that the interfacing doesn't show at the outer edges. The fusible will hold the seam allowances and slit opening in place.

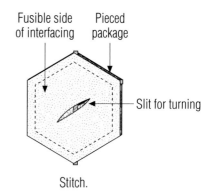

Fusible side of interfacing   Pieced package

Slit for turning

Stitch.

11. Referring to the photos on pages 96 and 98, position 3 packages on the left vest front; pin in place. Machine zigzag or blanket stitch around the finished edges of each box. Tack a small bow and tiny bell where the ribbons cross. Set the remaining package aside for the right front.

Blanket stitch (shown) or zigzag packages in place on left vest front.

✓ *Oh, Christmas Tree*

(Right Front)

MATERIALS

3" x 42" strip of green print
2 strips, each 3" x 42", of light fabric
Trim and ribbon for embellishment
Beads, bells, and charm or button for tree topper
60° triangle ruler

DIRECTIONS

1. For the treetop, Segment #1, place the tip of a 60° triangle ruler even with the top edge of the 3" x 42" green strip. Cut a small triangle.
2. Rotate the ruler 180° and place the 1" line of the ruler on the bottom edge of the strip. Cut Segment #2.
3. Rotate the ruler 180° and place the 2" line of the ruler along the top edge of the strip. Cut Segment #3.
4. Rotate the ruler 180° and place the 3" line along the bottom edge of the strip. Cut Segment #4.

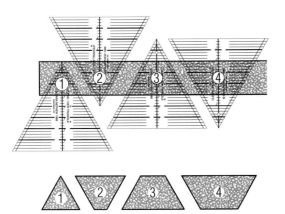

Cut 4 tree segments.

5. Fold and press each of the tree segments in half crosswise to crease-mark the center.

6. Cut a 1½" x 3" strip from the remaining green fabric for the tree trunk. Fold in half lengthwise and press to crease-mark the center.
7. Cut each 3"-wide light strip into 2 pieces, using the triangle ruler to cut the same angle on each side. You will have a total of 4 pieces.

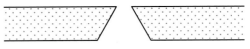

Make an angled cut in the center of light strips.

8. Sew a light strip to each end of Segment #1. Pin the pieces, right sides together, with points extending ¼" beyond each edge. Stitch ¼" from the raw edges and press the seams toward the triangle.

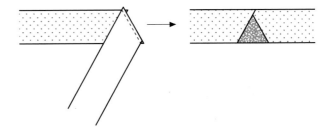

9. Using the crease mark as a guide, center the completed strip on the right front foundation, placing it 2" to 3" below the yoke line. Pin in place and trim the outer edges even with the foundation. Save the cutaways for the remainder of the Christmas tree.

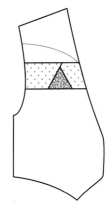

10. Add light strips to each end of the remaining tree segments as described in step 8, cutting an angle on any straight edges as described in step 7.

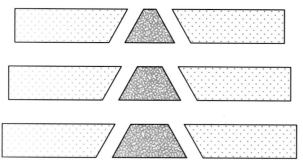

Add strips to remaining tree segments.

11. Sew a 3"-wide strip of light fabric to each long edge of the green trunk piece. Press the seams toward the trunk.

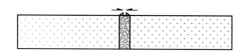

12. Center and pin the second tree segment strip to the bottom edge of the first with right sides together. Stitch ¼" from the raw edges. Flip the strip down onto the foundation; press and pin in place. Trim ends even with the foundation.

13. Repeat step 12 with the third and fourth tree-segment strips, adding the trunk strip last.

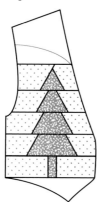

14. Cover the exposed foundation below the trunk with a strip of matching light fabric, using the stitch-and-flip method you used to attach the tree strips. Repeat above the tree to cover the foundation up to the yoke line. Trim even with the edges and the yoke line. Stitch ⅛" from all raw edges.

15. After adding "Christmas Presents" to the yoke (see below), trim the tree with beads, charms, and bells. Cover the raw edges at the yoke with trim. Stitch in place. To add a "French Knot Cascade" from the treetop down along the sides of the tree, follow the directions in step 4 on page 90 for the French Knot Twist. Use ⅛"- to ¼"-wide ribbon or trim. Tack a bow with long streamers to the treetop or add a special button or charm. Position the remaining package to the left of the tree. Stitch in place as you did on the left front.

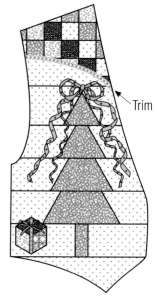

Trim

✓ Christmas Presents

(Front and Back Yokes)

Follow the directions for "Stepping-stones" on page 91, using four different fabrics with some color contrast. Feel free to experiment along the way to create a different patchwork pattern for the yokes.

✓ Vest Finishing

Follow the finishing directions for "Spring Has Sprung" on pages 92–94. If desired, make 2 buttonholes in the right front and sew buttons in place on the left front.

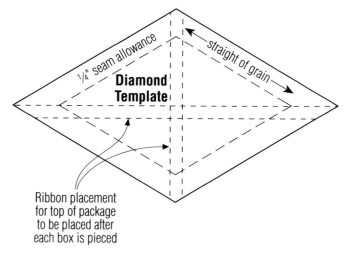

¼" seam allowance

straight of grain

Diamond Template

Ribbon placement for top of package to be placed after each box is pieced

Christmas Celebration
by Judy Murrah, Victoria, Texas, 1995.

Pink and green fabrics are a welcome adaptation of typical Christmas colors. Judy modified the size of "Oh, Christmas Tree" in this festive vest.

Seven Easy Pieces

- ◆ **Prairie Points 1**
- ◆ **Big Four Patch**
- ◆ **Flared Fan**
- ◆ **Large Log Cabin**
- ◆ **Little Triangle Squares**
- ◆ **Simple Seminole Patchwork**
- ◆ **Prairie Points 2**

✓ *Seven Easy Pieces Construction at a Glance*

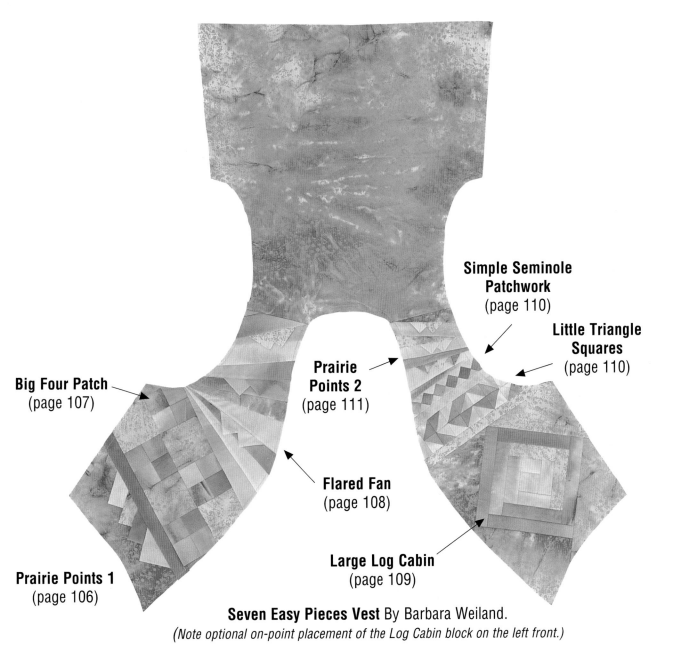

Simple Seminole Patchwork
(page 110)

Little Triangle Squares
(page 110)

Prairie Points 2
(page 111)

Big Four Patch
(page 107)

Flared Fan
(page 108)

Large Log Cabin
(page 109)

Prairie Points 1
(page 106)

Seven Easy Pieces Vest By Barbara Weiland.
(Note optional on-point placement of the Log Cabin block on the left front.)

PREPARATION

The back of this vest has no patchwork or embellishments, making it a quick-and-easy project.

Use a commercial vest pattern with styling similar to those shown in the photos, or use the body of Jacket Six from *Jacket Jazz Encore*. Set aside any facing pattern pieces, since you will not need them.

1. Cut 2 fronts and 1 back from muslin for the foundation and from the lining fabric.
2. Cut 1 vest back from the 1-yd. piece of fabric.
3. Cut and apply 2½"-wide strips of fusible interfacing to the wrong side of the foundation front as shown in step 1 on page 86.

Shopping List

All yardage requirements are based on 44"-wide fabrics, unless otherwise noted.

Vest Foundation	1¼ yds. muslin
Vest Lining, Fabric #1	1¼ yds. smooth cotton fabric*
Interfacing	¼ yd. lightweight fusible interfacing
Vest Back, Fabric #3	1 yd. (You will use some of this in the patchwork.)
Patchwork Fabrics #1–6	⅓ yd. each of 4 additional fabrics**
Piping	3 to 4 yds. for outer-edge finish**
Elastic	6" to 8" long for back (optional)
Assorted charms, beads, braids, studs, etc.	To embellish vest as desired

*Or use leftover fabric from patchwork pieces.

**You may finish the vest with piping or bias binding around the outer edges. If you decide to do this, consider piping the seams between the various patchwork elements as you add them to the foundation. Refer to the vest photo on page 113. For bias binding, purchase an additional ⅓ yd. of one of the fabrics. For piping, you will need 3 to 4 yds., depending on the vest size and shape.

✓ Prairie Points 1

(Right Front)

MATERIALS

Fabric #1 for lower bottom background
4" x 12" strip of Fabrics #3 and #4
Piping

DIRECTIONS

1. Place a strip of Fabric #1 on the lower right corner of the right vest front foundation, positioning it at the desired angle. This will be the background for Prairie Points 1. The angle will dictate the angle of the entire right vest front. It also dictates how much Flared Fan fill-in you will need later. Pin in place, trim excess even with the raw edges of the foundation, and stitch ⅛" from the raw edge.

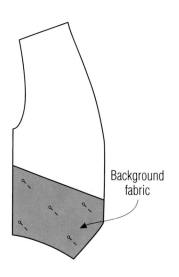

Background fabric

2. Cut 3 squares, each 3" x 3" or 4" x 4", from Fabrics #3 and #4, for a total of 6 squares.

3. Fold fabric squares in half on the diagonal from Point #1 to Point #2. Fold in half again so the resulting folded triangle is 1½" (or 2" wide at the raw edges if you started with a 4" square). Press.

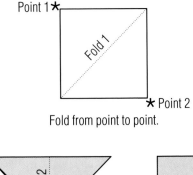

Fold from point to point.

Make a second fold.

4. Position as many as 6 Prairie Points 1 on the foundation, aligning the raw edges with the top raw edge of Fabric #1 and overlapping the points as needed. Pin in place.

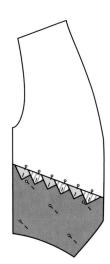

Pin Prairie Points to background fabric.

5. If you wish, add a 1½"-wide strip of a contrasting fabric above the Prairie Points 1 as seen in the vests on pages 105 and 113. Pin the strip in place face down on top of the points with raw edges even. Stitch ¼" from the raw edges, then flip the strip up onto the foundation; press and pin in place. Trim ends even with the foundation.

Note: For added interest, pipe the seams between each patchwork piece on both vest fronts.

✓Big Four Patch

(Right Front)

MATERIALS

2" x 42" strip each of Fabrics #3 and #4
3½" x 42" strip of Fabric #2

DIRECTIONS

1. Cut the 2"-wide strips in half crosswise to make 4 equal strips. Set 1 strip of each fabric aside for the Flared Fan (page 108).

2. Sew the remaining pieces together, using a ¼"-wide seam allowance. Press the seam toward the darker fabric. Crosscut into 10 segments, each 2" wide.

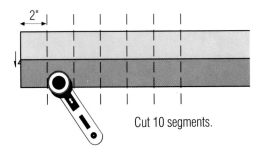

Cut 10 segments.

3. Arrange the segments in four-patch units as shown and sew together, matching the seams carefully. Press.

Make 5.

4. From Fabric #2, cut 5 squares, each 3½" x 3½".

5. Alternate the four-patch units with the plain squares in 2 rows. Sew the pieces together in rows, pressing the seams in opposite directions from row to row.

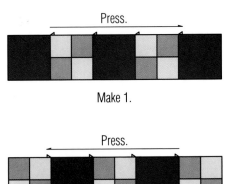

Press.

Make 1.

Press.

Make 1.

6. Sew one of the rows to the top edge of the Prairie Points 1 (or the divider strip above it), using the stitch-and-flip method. Add the remaining row in the same manner, pinning carefully so the seams match. Flip up onto the patchwork; press, pin in place, and trim edges even with the foundation. If necessary, add a small piece, trimmed from the first row to the second row, to cover the foundation completely.

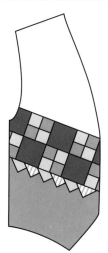

✓Flared Fan

(Right Front)

MATERIALS

2" x 22" strip each of Fabrics #1–#6

DIRECTIONS

1. Position the first fabric strip at the upper edge of the Big Four Patch, right sides together and raw edges even. Stitch ¼" from the raw edges; flip up onto the foundation; press, trim, and pin. At the seam line, identify the lower left corner of the strip as A and the upper right corner as B.

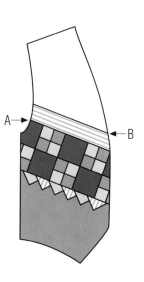

2. Position the next strip, right sides together, shifting the raw edge down toward A as shown. Pin and stitch. Fold the foundation out of the way and trim the first strip even with the raw-edge of the second strip. Flip the second strip up onto foundation. Pin. Trim the ends even with the foundation edges.

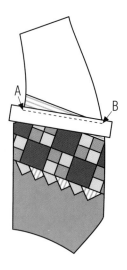

3. Repeat step 2 with the 4 remaining strips until the right-front foundation is covered. The last strips can be wider if you want to make a larger area to embellish with Prairie Points 1 or studs.

◆ **Note:** If you had any Prairie Points 1 left over or want to make more, you can insert them in the seam between two strips in the upper shoulder area as shown in the vest photos on pages 105 and 113.

4. Stitch ⅛" from the raw edges around the right front. Press and set aside.

✓Large Log Cabin

(Left Front)

MATERIALS

2½" square of Fabric #3
2" x 42" strip each of Fabrics #2, #4, #5, and #6

DIRECTIONS

1. Divide the fabric strips into 2 contrasting sets; for example, dark and light, pink and blue, or prints and solids, depending on your fabric choices. You will use 1 set to piece the top and left sides of the center square, and the remaining set for the bottom and right sides of the center square. (If you do not have contrasting sets, just use 2 fabrics, one for each set of the square's adjacent corners as shown in the photo on page 104.)

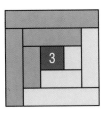

2. Center the 2½" square of Fabric #3 on the lower left front so that it is equidistant from the front and side edges and the bottom edge, excluding the point.

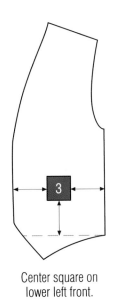

Center square on
lower left front.

3. Decide on the order of the 2 fabrics in each set. Pin the first strip of Set #1, right side down, along the right raw edge of the center square on the foundation. Stitch ¼" from the raw edge. Flip onto the foundation; press and pin in place. Trim excess fabric strip even with the raw edges of the center square. Adding strips in numerical order around the center square, sew a strip of the same fabric across the bottom of the first strip and the square.

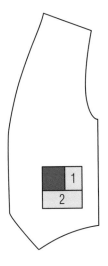

4. Repeat step 3 with a strip of Fabric #1 from Set #2 for the left edge and top of the center square.
5. Use the second fabric from Set #1 for the next 2 strips, followed by the second fabric from Set #2 for the 2 remaining strips. If necessary, add a strip to the bottom edge of the last strip to cover the vest point.

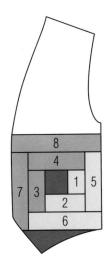

Add strips in order
around the square.

✔ Little Triangle Squares

(Left Front)

MATERIALS

2" x 28" strip each of Fabrics #2 and #3
1" to 2"-wide strip of Fabric #6

DIRECTIONS

1. On the lighter of Fabrics #2 and #3, mark 2" intervals on the wrong side. These will be cutting lines later. Draw a zigzag line from corner to opposite corner of each marked square. These are stitching and cutting guides.

Mark on wrong side of lighter fabric strip.

2. Pin the Fabric #2 and Fabric #3 strips right sides together. Stitch ¼" away from the diagonal lines on each side, taking 1 stitch over the raw edge, then pivoting the strip so you can stitch the entire piece on one side of the line without stopping. Repeat for the other side of the line.

Stitch ¼" away from diagonal line in a zigzag manner.

3. Cut into 14 squares on the vertical lines. Cut the squares along the lines between the rows of stitching for a total of 28 pieced squares. Press the seams toward the darker fabric in each square.

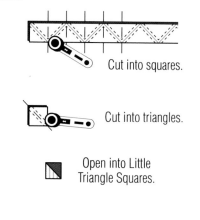

Cut into squares.

Cut into triangles.

Open into Little Triangle Squares.

4. Arrange the squares in 2 or 3 rows, experimenting with the designs you can make. When you are pleased with your arrangement, sew the squares together in rows long enough to reach across the vest above the Log Cabin. Press the seams in opposite directions from row to row. Sew each row in place above the Log Cabin, using the stitch-and-flip method. Add a 1"- to 2"-wide strip of Fabric #6 above the Little Triangle Squares.

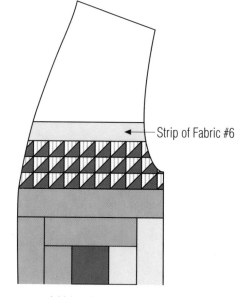

◄— Strip of Fabric #6

Add 2 or 3 rows of
Little Triangle Squares.

✔ Simple Seminole Patchwork

(Left Front)

MATERIALS

1½" x 29" strip of Fabric #1
1¼" x 29" strip of Fabric #4
1½" x 29" strip of Fabric #3

DIRECTIONS

1. Sew the 3 strips together in the order shown, using ¼"-wide seam allowances. Press the seams toward the darker fabric. Crosscut into 1¼"-wide segments.

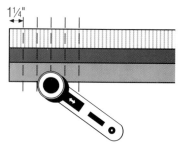

2. Sew the segments together, offsetting each piece as shown and using ¼"-wide seams. Sew enough segments together to fit across the vest above the Fabric #6 strip. Trim away the peaks along the top and bottom edges as shown, making sure that there is ¼" above and below the inner tip of the center row of squares for seam allowances.

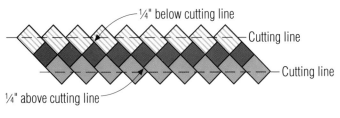

¼" below cutting line

Cutting line

Cutting line

¼" above cutting line

Offset as shown.

3. Sew the Seminole strip to the vest, using the stitch-and-flip method. Flip, press, and pin. Make 2 more rows of patchwork and add them above the first row. You can create different designs by turning the rows, rather than stitching them all on the same way. Play with them before stitching each one in place.

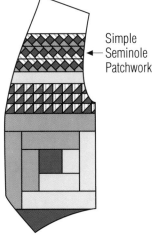

Simple Seminole Patchwork

✓*Prairie Points 2*

(Left Front)

MATERIALS

3" or 4" square each of Fabrics #3 and #4

DIRECTIONS

1. Fold each square in half, wrong sides together, to make a rectangle. Fold each short end to the center (B). Press. The open side is the right side of Prairie Point 2.

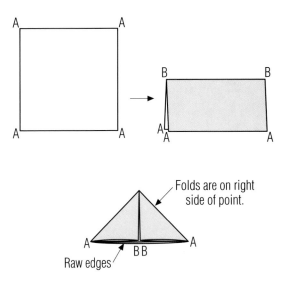

Folds are on right side of point.

Raw edges

2. Cover the remainder of the foundation on the left front with strips of various widths, stitching them straight across or adding them as described for the "Flared Fan" on page 108. Insert 2 Prairie Points 2 in the seams between 2 strips in the upper shoulder area.

3. Trim all patchwork even with the foundation if necessary and stitch ⅛" from all raw edges.

4. Embellish the patchwork as desired. Refer to the vest photos on pages 104, 105, and 113 for ideas.

✓*Vest Finishing*

If you wish to pipe the outer edges of your vest, refer to "Vest Finishing" on page 92. If you prefer to bind the edges, follow the steps below.

1. Place the vest back face up on the vest back foundation and pin in place so you can treat the two layers as one. (Adding the foundation helps balance the weight of the embellished fronts with the vest back.) Stitch the vest fronts to the vest back at the shoulders and side seams; press the seams open.

2. Stitch the vest front lining to the vest back lining at the shoulder and side seams. Press the seams open.

3. Place the lining and vest *wrong sides together* and pin the raw edges together. Stitch ⅝" from the raw edges. Trim ½", leaving ⅛" of fabric beyond the stitching.

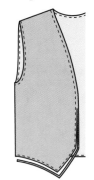

Trim ⅛" from stitching.

4. Cut 2"-wide bias strips from the binding fabric. Join the short bias strips to make one piece long enough to finish the other edge of the vest. Press seams open. Fold the strip in half lengthwise, wrong sides together, and press. Open the strip and press under ¼" at one end. Refold.

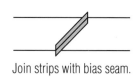

Join strips with bias seam.

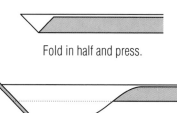

Fold in half and press.

Turn under ¼".

◆ **Note:** If you prefer to make one continuous strip of bias binding, follow the directions for cutting continuous binding on page 81 of *Jacket Jazz*.

5. Pin the raw edges of binding *to the lining side of the vest*, beginning and ending at the center of the lower back edge and overlapping the ends as shown. Stitch ¼" from the raw edges, mitering the corners at the vest points as shown above right.

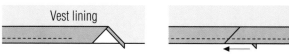

Vest lining

Tuck cut end into open end.

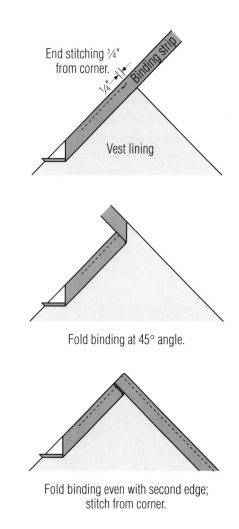

End stitching ¼" from corner.

Binding strip

Vest lining

Fold binding at 45° angle.

Fold binding even with second edge; stitch from corner.

6. Turn the binding to the right side of the vest; press and pin in place. Edgestitch through all layers.

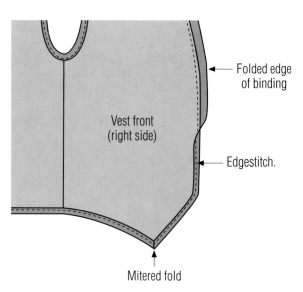

Folded edge of binding

Vest front (right side)

Edgestitch.

Mitered fold

Seven Easy Pieces *by Judy Murrah,*
Victoria, Texas, 1994.

There's lots of room for embellishment on this easy vest. With a plain back, the vest is a good one-day project for an experienced quiltmaker or seamstress.

Bias Appliqué Tabard

A tabard is a loose-fitting, vest-type garment that has no side seams. The only seams are at the shoulders, so the sewing is easy and there is no fitting. The style is attractive on all figures. With so many colors in the fabrics, the tabard will coordinate with a variety of tops, skirts, or pants. And the best thing is, it won't take long to make.

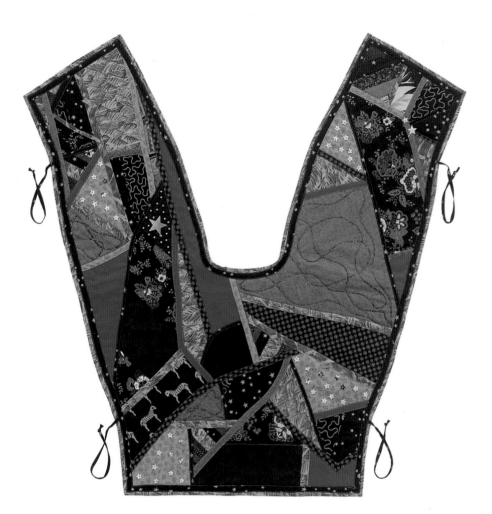

Bias Appliqué Tabard by Judy Murrah.

PREPARATION

1. The pullout pattern at the back of this book includes the cutting lines for 5 different sizes. Determine which size pattern to use and trace the appropriately sized pattern pieces onto pattern tracing paper or cloth. Lengthen 2" to 3" at the lengthen/shorten lines for a longer tabard or even more for a knee-length tunic.

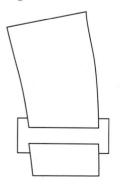

2. Cut the tabard fronts and back from the lining and foundation fabrics. Sew the tabard foundation fronts to the back at the shoulders, *using ¹/₂"-wide seam allowances.* Repeat with the lining pieces. Press all seams open.

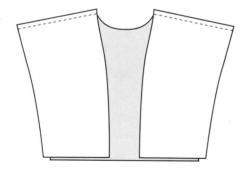

Shopping List

Foundation	⅔ to 1¼ yds. muslin*
Lining	⅔ to 1¼ yds. smooth cotton fabric*
Patchwork	¼ yd. each of 7 or 8 fabrics or scraps of fabric from your scrap bag, more for a tunic length
Bias Binding	⅓ yd. each of 2 different fabrics to finish outer edges
Decorative Thread, Yarn, and/or Ribbon	For couching trims in place or for random couching in patches
Embellishments	Assorted beads, sequins, charms, and buttons

*The yardage requirement is dependent on the size of the pattern pieces. You will need more fabric for the foundation if you decide to lengthen the pattern. To determine how much fabric you need, do a trial pattern layout at home, using your traced (and adjusted) pattern pieces. You can cut the front and back lining pieces from different fabrics in your stash if you wish.

In addition to the fabrics and notions listed, you will also need these special supplies:
    Bias-tape maker
    Spray adhesive in a can

PREPARATION (CONT.)

3. Pin the foundation to the lining, *wrong sides together.*
    Stitch ⅛" from all raw edges.

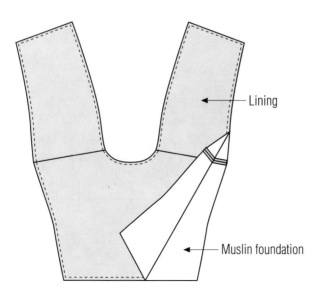

Lining

Muslin foundation

DIRECTIONS

1. Working outside or in a well-ventilated room, apply a light coating of spray adhesive to the right side of the foundation. Place the adhesive-coated tabard on a flat surface where you can leave it undisturbed until it is covered with fabric pieces.

2. If you purchased ¼-yd. pieces of fabric for this project, cut them into random shapes with straight edges. If you are working from your scrap bag or stash, choose coordinating fabric scraps. I just put my scraps in a heap next to the flat tabard and start pulling pieces. It's somewhat like working a jigsaw puzzle. It's fun, so let go and let the child in you play with the scraps. For the first fabric, choose a rather large piece that will go from the back over the shoulder, establishing a point where you can integrate all remaining pieces for a unified look. Smooth it in place, right side up, on the foundation fabric, making sure there are no wrinkles.

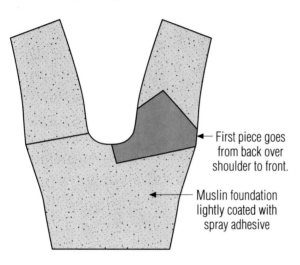

← First piece goes from back over shoulder to front.

← Muslin foundation lightly coated with spray adhesive

Note: You do not need pins to hold the pieces in place. If necessary, you can easily lift and reposition pieces as you work, but too much of this will cause the adhesive to wear out. If that happens, use a few pins to keep the pieces in place.

3. Continue to select and add fabric pieces or scraps to cover the entire foundation, making sure that the pieces butt up to each other or overlap by ⅛". You will cover all raw edges with bias later. That means that the smaller your pieces are, the more bias you will have to stitch in place. As you work, make sure to keep the piece balanced, using the same fabrics in somewhat equal amounts on the front and back.

4. Fill a bobbin with thread that contrasts with or matches the lining, and straight-stitch ⅛" from all raw edges of each piece. This stitching will show on the lining side of the completed tabard.

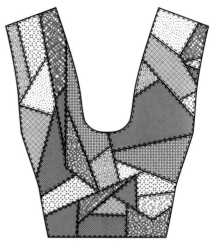

Straight-stitch each piece to foundation and lining.

5. Embellish the larger, simpler fabric areas with decorative machine stitches and/or textured and colored yarns, ribbons, and threads. This is an easy and attractive way to add texture and dimension, as well as color and unique detail to an area. Try decorative bobbin stitching or machine couching as described in the sidebar on page 119.

6. Make bias tape in different widths from a variety of fabrics. Begin with a square of fabric, at least 12" square. Mark the center of each of the 2 opposite edges with a pin. Fold the square in half on the diagonal and press; cut in half on the crease line.

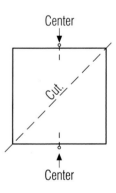

7. With right sides together and the pin-marked edges even, sew the resulting triangles together, using a ¼"-wide seam allowance. When properly positioned for stitching, the 2 pieces look like a giant tooth. Press the seam open.

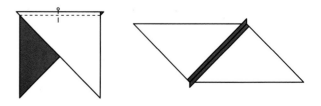

✓ *Decorative Stitch Embellishments*

- **Decorative Bobbin Stitching**—Choose special threads, cords, or ribbons and hand wind them onto the bobbin. Thin, smooth yarns without slubs or bumps will work too. When you thread the bobbin case or drop in your bobbin, bypass the tension guide, bringing the thread up through the hole in the throat plate in the normal way. Your sewing-machine dealer can tell you how to adjust your machine for this type of stitching. *It's a good idea to experiment with this technique on scraps before you begin the tabard.*

  For the top thread, choose one that matches or contrasts with the decorative thread in the bobbin. It will be more or less visible on the top of the special thread.

  Begin by placing the tabard on the bed of the machine so you will be stitching in the area you wish to embellish. To find it easily, put a pin in the right side so you can find the stitching that outlines it on the lining side. Stitch with a long straight stitch or an open decorative stitch, staying within the area outlined by the stitching. Begin and end at a stitching line, then pull the threads through to the right side and tie them. Bias will cover the knots later. Depending on the thread and the stitch you use, this stitching sometimes looks like it was done by hand.

- **Machine Couching**—You can also add threads to the surface of the tabard by stitching over them from the top. In this case, you arrange the decorative thread, ribbon, or cord in the area you wish to embellish and stitch over it with another thread, using a regular zigzag setting. For this technique, you can use textured yarns and decorative threads that might not work in the

"Decorative Bobbin Stitching" described above. If your sewing machine has built-in embroidery stitches, try them too. Use a decorative thread, such as rayon machine-embroidery or metallic thread, on top and regular thread in the bobbin. A contrast in texture and color adds more interest to the finished work. If you want only the decorative yarn to show, use a matching thread.

Use an all-purpose sewing foot or cording foot. Adjust your sewing machine's zigzag-width setting to just clear the width of the decorative yarn or thread you will stitch over. To begin, pull about 3" of yarn behind the foot and begin to stitch, zigzagging over the yarn, holding it taut in front of the foot. The needle and presser foot will do the work as you keep the yarn centered under the foot. If your machine has a couching/braiding foot, use it. It holds the yarn in front of the foot, freeing your hands for maneuvering the fabric. Leave a tail of yarn at the end of the couching to thread through a large needle, bring to the other side, and tie off.

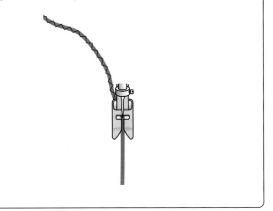

8. Mark lines the width you want to cut the bias strips. For a ¼"-wide finished bias, mark lines ½" apart. For a ½"-wide bias, mark rows 1" apart. The last row marked may be narrower than the others. Trim it away and discard.

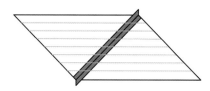

9. Pin the parallelogram together to form a tube, allowing one of the marked widths to hang off each end and making sure the marked lines match. *When properly pinned, this tube will not lie flat.* Stitch and press the seam open. Cut along the line for a continuous bias strip.

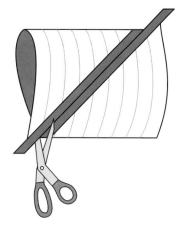

10. Turn under and press the long raw edges of each bias strip. Finished bias should be no wider than ½". To make this step faster and easier, use a bias-tape maker or use bias bars to make finished fabric tubes as shown for the "Woven String Strips" in step 7 on page 62.

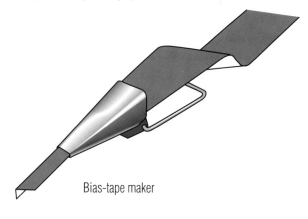

Bias-tape maker

11. Center bias strips over butted raw edges of the patchwork pieces on the tabard. Pin in place. Stitch the bias strips in place close to each folded edge. If you have an edgestitching foot for your machine, this is the perfect place to use it.

Note: Pin a whole section of bias before you start to stitch. This way, you are less likely to sew a strip of bias down before you have sewn strips that intersect with it. When bias comes to a dead end, it should be covered by another piece of finished bias or end at an outer edge.

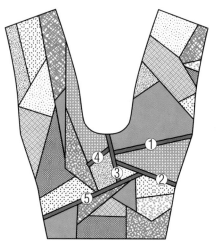

Strips #1, #2, and #4 go under
Strip #3 before stitching #3 in place.
Strip #3 goes under Strip #5,
and Strip #5 goes under Strip #2
before stitching.

✓Tabard Finishing

1. Using the fabric purchased for the outer edge finish, cut bias strips 1¼" wide. Using the other ⅓-yard piece of fabric for the inner edge finish, cut bias strips 1" wide. Turn under the raw edges of the narrower strip so that it is ½" wide.

½"

2. Turn under and press ¼" at one end of the 1¼"-wide bias strip as shown.

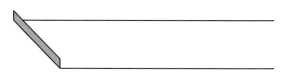

3. Beginning at the lower edge of the back and with right sides together, pin the 1¼"-wide bias to the lining side of the tabard. Keep raw edges even, overlapping the ends at the center back. Cut away excess bias. Stitch ¼" from the raw edges, mitering the corners as you reach them. (Refer to the mitering directions on page 112.)

4. Turn the bias to the right side of the tabard, encasing the raw edges. Pin the bias in place, folding in the mitered corners.

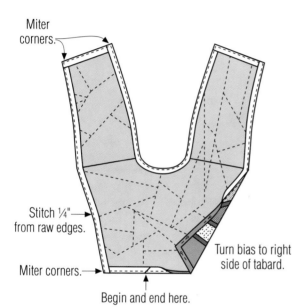

Miter corners.

Stitch ¼" from raw edges.

Miter corners.

Turn bias to right side of tabard.

Begin and end here.

5. Stitch in-the-ditch of the seam *on the lining side* to catch the raw edge in place on the right side. This is easier than trying to stitch close to the raw edge on the right side.

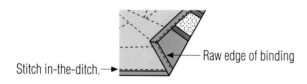

Stitch in-the-ditch.

Raw edge of binding

6. For ties, cut 4 bias strips, each 1" x 12". Turn under and press ¼" on the long raw edges. Fold in half lengthwise, wrong sides together, and stitch close to the edge. Tie a knot at the end of each tie.

7. On the right side of the tabard, pin the tie ends to the front and back sides at the marks given on the pattern, aligning the ends with the raw edge of the bias binding.

Note: If you lengthened the tabard pattern for a longer version, try it on and mark your waistline position. Attach ties at this location.

8. Using the machine stitching on the bias binding as a guide, position the 1"-wide strips of bias (with edges turned under) over the raw edges of the bias binding. Pin in place, mitering the corners. Stitch close to both edges.

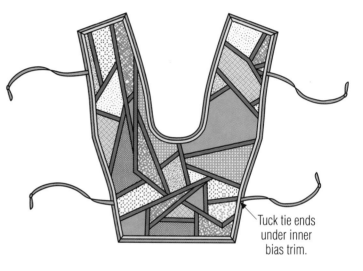

Tuck tie ends under inner bias trim.

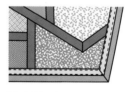

Stitch bias in place over raw edge of outer bias.

9. Embellish the tabard with beads, sequins, charms, buttons, etc. Tie bows at the side seams and wear the finished tabard over your favorite blouse and skirt for your next fabric-shopping expedition.

Waste Not,
Want Not Tabard

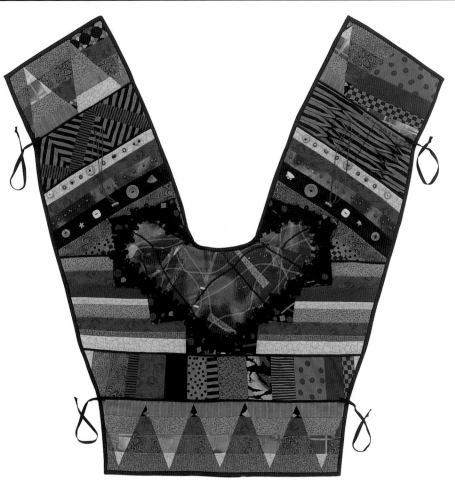

Waste Not, Want Not Tabard by Judy Murrah.

DIRECTIONS

1. Prepare the foundation and lining as directed in steps 1–3 on pages 116–17 for the "Bias Appliqué Tabard."
2. Look through your selection of leftover pieces.
   - Are there any strips long enough to cover the back and 2 fronts?
   - Are there 2 matching or closely similar pieces that you could place opposite each other on the fronts? Are there 2 different techniques that are similar in color and/or fabric that could be used in the same way?
   - Is there a large piece that could be cut into a yoke to extend over the shoulders from the back?
   - Are there any squares that could be folded for Prairie Points to insert in a seam?
   - Are there several fabric strips long enough that you could sew them together and use on both fronts to show case buttons or charms?

     Continue thinking this way and placing strips and groups of pieces on the foundation until you are happy with the arrangement. Refer to the photo above for ideas. If necessary, make additional patchwork, using any of the techniques in this book or those in *Jacket Jazz* and *Jacket Jazz Encore*.
3. Apply the pieces to the tabard. To make it easier to handle, make a numbered sketch of the tabard layout and attach a numbered label to the corresponding piece for reference as you work. Then remove the pieces and begin stitching them in place.

Shopping List

Foundation	⅔ to 1¼ yds. muslin*
Lining	⅔ to 1¼ yds. smooth cotton fabric*
Fabric for Single-Fold Bias Binding	⅓ yd.
Leftover Patchwork and Fabric Strips	
Piping	3 yds.
Embellishments	Buttons, beads, ribbons, and other trims as desired

*Your yardage requirement is dependent on the size of the pattern pieces. Do a trial layout at home, using fabric from your stash.

---

4. Begin at the bottom edge of the back or the fronts and pin the correct piece in place. Trim patchwork even with the foundation as needed. Flip the tabard over and stitch ⅛" from the foundation edge.

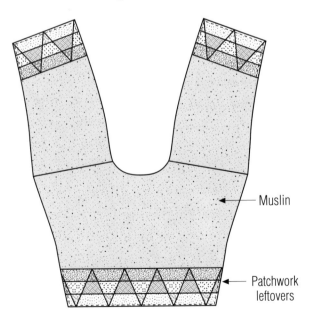

Muslin

Patchwork leftovers

5. To pipe between the pieces, pin the piping raw edge even with the unstitched edge of the first piece. Use a zipper foot to stitch close to the cord.

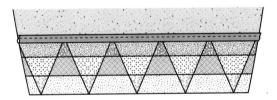

6. Place the next piece of patchwork face down on top of the first with raw edges even. Stitch next to the piping cord. Flip the patchwork up onto the foundation; press and pin in place. Continue adding pieces or strips in this manner until the entire surface is covered. To define the shoulder seam, add piping, then continue adding pieces to the back or front until the entire foundation is covered.

Tabard Finishing

1. Cut 2"-wide bias strips from the binding fabric and join the strips to make one continuous piece. If you prefer to cut a continuous strip of bias, refer to the directions on pages 119–20 or follow the method on page 81 in *Jacket Jazz*. Fold the binding strip in half, wrong sides together, and press. Open one end; turn under and press ¼"; refold.

2. Beginning on the lining side at the center back, pin the binding to the tabard with raw edges even. Stitch, mitering the corners as shown on page 112 and tucking the end into the bias at the point where you started. Turn the bias over the raw edges to encase them and pin the folded edge in place, folding in mitered corners. Machine stitch close to the folded edge.

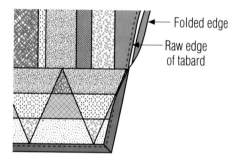

Folded edge

Raw edge of tabard

3. Make ties for the sides of the tabard as described in step 6 in "Tabard Finishing" on page 121. Turn under 1" at the unknotted end of each tie and tack in position on the tabard fronts and back.

1"

Turn under end.

4. Embellish the tabard with your choice of embellishments—beads, buttons, ribbons, charms, and trim.

Silk Tie Tabard

Here's a great way to use up discarded men's ties. Check with your sweetheart before you "rescue" any of his. Better yet, keep your eyes out for bargain ties at estate sales and consignment shops. Make sure you choose clean ties with little visible wear. This is a really easy project and could cost little or nothing, depending on your source for the ties. Directions are for a waist-length tabard only.

Silk Tie Tabard by Judy Murrah.

✓*Shopping List*

All yardage requirements listed are based on 44"-wide fabrics, unless otherwise noted.

Foundation	²/₃ to 1¹/₄ yds. muslin*
Lining	²/₃ to 1¹/₄ yds. smooth cotton*
Ties	7 to 10 men's neckties in designs and colors that work well together
Binding	¹/₃ yd. coordinating fabric
Braid	5 yds. of ¹/₂"-wide coordinating trim
Thread	Coordinating color for decorative stitching and clear monofilament
Embellishments (optional)	

   *Your yardage requirement is dependent on the size of the pattern pieces. Do a trial layout at home, using fabrics from your stash.

DIRECTIONS

1. Prepare the foundation and lining as directed for the "Bias Appliqué Tabard," steps 1–3, on pages 116–17.

2. Remove the tie labels and undo the stitching along the center back of each tie. Discard the interfacing (or save it to make a tie of your own or one for your special guy).

3. Select the 3 ties you plan to use on the tabard back. Press the ties flat to remove creases, leaving the outer edges turned under and point facings still attached. Open out and press the seams flat on the remaining ties. Remove the facings at both ends of these ties.

Leave outer edges turned under on 3 ties.

Open out and press flat.
Remove facings.

4. Place the tabard on a flat surface with the muslin side face up. Using the ties selected and prepared for the tabard back, center the large end of the center tie (#1) on the tabard back foundation with the wide point ending 1½" above the bottom edge. Pin in place and trim the excess tie fabric even with the neckline.

5. Position a tie on each side of the first one with the point 1½" from the bottom edge. Depending on the size of the ties and the size of the tabard pattern you are using, you will need to overlap 2 outside ties with the center tie or leave a space between them, or have them just touching as shown in the illustration below. Bring the ties over the shoulders to the center front corners. Pin in place and trim even with the foundation edges.

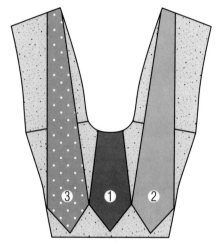

Place a tie on each side
of the first one.

6. Cover the exposed muslin between the 3 ties with one of the remaining ties, dividing this tie into 2 pieces. If the space is too large for one tie to cover both areas, then use 2 similar ties. Place the raw edges of these pieces under the finished edges of the first 3 ties you placed. Pin in place and trim even with the foundation.

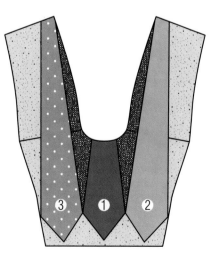

7. Use another tie to cover the exposed foundation below the tie points. You may need to sew 2 ties together for this. Pin in place; trim even with the foundation.

8. Use the remaining ties to cover any remaining exposed foundation. If one tie on each side is not large enough to cover the space, add another one. Place the raw edges under the turned edges of Ties #2 and #3. Pin in place and trim even with the foundation. Stitch ⅛" from all raw edges. Remove the pins.

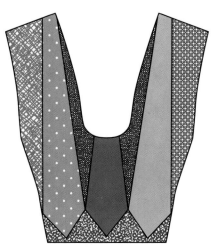

Cover the remainder
of fronts and backs.

9. Thread your machine with clear monofilament thread on top and regular thread in the bobbin. Adjust the tension as needed. Stitch close to the finished edge of Ties #1, #2, and #3 to anchor them to the tabard.

10. Using a decorative machine stitch and contrasting thread, stitch next to the finished edge of Ties #1, #2, and #3. If you prefer, you can do fancy hand-embroidered stitches in place of the decorative machine stitching. Further embellish the ties with Silk-Ribbon Embroidery (pages 79–81), Decorative Bobbin Stitching, or Machine Couching (page 119) if you wish.

Tabard Finishing

1. Cut 1¼"-wide bias strips from the binding fabric and sew them together into one piece long enough to go around the outer edges of the tabard. If you prefer, you may use the method on page 81 of *Jacket Jazz* to cut a continuous strip of bias. (Do not fold the bias and press.)

2. Apply the flat bias to the outer edges of the tabard, following steps 2–5 of "Tabard Finishing" on pages 120–21.

3. Make ties as directed in step 6 of "Tabard Finishing" and attach to the tabard as directed in step 7.

4. Beginning at the center back bottom edge, position braid trim along the stitching that secures the raw edge of the binding on the right side of the tabard and stitch in place. Miter the corners and turn under the end when you reach the starting point.

5. Add other embellishments if you wish.

You're finished! I hope you've had fun exploring all the new techniques and garment shapes I've included. I'll be on the watch for you in your jazzy new outfits.

Judy Murrah's enthusiasm for designing and sharing her designs for wonderful wearables continues in this, her third book. With new ideas and tricks to try, plus previous ones to re-explore, she keeps busy teaching classes for shops, quilt guilds, and at regional seminars throughout the country. Since she can't be everywhere to share her new designs, Judy graciously provides directions for making them in her books and through her monthly Mystery Jacket correspondence courses. Judy's original wearables, including some of the Fairfield Fashion Show garments she's designed, also have been featured in various quilting publications. Judy's growth as a professional instructor and designer has paralleled her responsibilities as Director of Education for Quilts, Inc., the Houston company that produces the successful Quilt Market/Quilt Festival shows.

Judy is a proud native Texan, born and reared in San Antonio. She lives in Victoria, Texas, with her husband, Tom, and visits her three young adult children in other parts of Texas.